Mary Helen Campbell

Sundays in Yoho

Twelve Stories for Children And Their Friends

Mary Helen Campbell

Sundays in Yoho
Twelve Stories for Children And Their Friends

ISBN/EAN: 9783337004316

Printed in Europe, USA, Canada, Australia, Japan

Cover: Foto ©Thomas Meinert / pixelio.de

More available books at **www.hansebooks.com**

Sundays

in

Yoho.

TWELVE STORIES FOR CHILDREN AND THEIR FRIENDS.

EDITED BY

MARY HELEN CAMPBELL.

" And without a parable spake he not unto them."—St. Matthew xii. 34.

Montreal:

WILLIAM DRYSDALE & CO.

1884.

PN
6071
C5C3

PRINTED BY GAZETTE PRINTING COMPANY, MONTREAL.

In

LOVING MEMORY

OF

Two Little Worshippers

WHOSE

SERVICE IS PERFECT

IN THE CHURCH ABOVE.

PREFACE.

Yoho is an island in one of the small northern lakes of Ontario, only to be found depicted on local charts and unmentioned, so far as I know, in any gazetteer. Yet it has a certain quiet celebrity of its own which it is far from being my desire to make public. Life on the island is a return to first principles, a child life in the best and wisest sense. Children form a large element in its limited population and in that of the adjoining islands. Those who are no longer children in years, even to grandsires and granddames, are still such in heart, and find their chief happiness in the children's joys. The first day of the week is there the holy of the Lord and honourable, but it is also a delight. At the hour appointed for morning service, cottages and tents send forth their occupants while, in all directions, from neighbouring islets and from settlers' clearings upon the mainland, boats large and small bring their quota of worshippers into the quiet harbour. The chapel in which they meet is one of nature's building, a pleasant hollow among mossy rocks and boulders, overshaded by spreading maples and hemlocks. Saucy squirrels have been known to gambol and chatter among the branches over the preacher's head, stray bees and beetles to cause a temporary flutter in the choir, and the silly chuckle or mournful wail of the loon to excite the indignation of the otherwise well-behaved dogs. But generally all nature is in harmony with the spirit of the day and helpful to devotion. The children are there expectant. They are waiting for the new story, a story they can remember and tell and give the meaning of and lay up in their hearts for many days. Woe to the reverend divine, however pious, learned, and eloquent he may be, if he disappoint them. With that congregation his reputation as a preacher is gone forever.

From among the sermons which the children like and which their elder brothers and sisters, their fathers and mothers remember also, I have chosen twelve for publication. Some of them have been delivered more than once to varying audiences in the chapel of Yoho, and, unless by special request as sometimes happens, cannot be repeated there. But the young people wish to have them in a book of their own, and perhaps there are other boys and girls in the world to whom the stories may give pleasure and do good. My critical young friends who have heard them spoken extempore will doubtless detect many variations from the original in form of expression, but in their main features they will find the narratives unchanged. It is not my duty to provoke or to disarm general criticism of the productions of others which it has been my office simply to collect and arrange. They pleased and profited the children and me and will do the same, I trust, to those who are like-minded.

THE EDITOR.

MONTREAL, Christmas 1884.

CONTENTS.

I.

The Story of Orion.

I.

The Story of Orion.

" But unto you that fear my name shall the Sun of righteousness arise with healing in his wings."—MALACHI, iv. 2.

When looking up some bright winter evening into our clear
northern sky, you have seen three large stars in a perfect
line, and, hanging from them as it were, a long hazy cluster
like a comet's tail. These are the belt and sword of Orion,
the mighty hunter. You can trace his form as it is marked
by other stars above and below the girdle, and farther down
in the southern heavens are the hunter's dogs, the greater
and the less, that follow him in the nightly chase.

Who was Orion? Ages ago, the story tells us, when Europe was a wilderness and no human foot trod the soil of
this western world, he came, a giant and a slayer of wild
beasts, to the beautiful island of Chios, to the court of its
wise king, Oenopion. He came to one of the loveliest spots
in the old world, the fairest isle in the sparkling Ægean sea,
a little land of green pastures and flowing waters, of vine-
clad hills and snow-capped mountains, of waving cornfields
and evergreen glades. Such grapes as flourished there grew
nowhere else in the world ; citrons and almonds, pomegra-
nates and palms, with many another tree which was pleasant
to the eye and whose fruit was good for food, stocked its
orchards, or, untended by man, cheered the traveller by the
wayside ; and from its mountain quarries came the pure
white Chian marble fit for the palace of the greatest king.

In such a paradise there was everything to make Orion happy. Good king Oenopion loved the giant hunter and, as the greatest token of his affection, gave him for wife his daughter Merope. For a time Orion acted well, but the time was very brief. Evil thoughts came into his mind, proud feelings swelled his heart, and wicked deeds soon followed them. He rebelled against the king and ill-treated his daughter; he destroyed the fertile plains which it was his duty to protect, and made the peaceful, happy reign a time of strife and wretchedness. Oenopion was grieved. He would fain have forgiven the rebel, but without repentance forgiveness could only lead to greater sins on the part of Orion and greater injury to the king's land and people. So with a sad heart the good monarch banished the giant from court and city, from field and orchard, away to the dreary seashore, there to wait until some passing ship should call to take him to a far off country.

So all unarmed Orion sat down upon the yellow sands, not daring to return to the palace or even to enter the groves and meadows that skirted the beach, for he knew that the king's trusty soldiers barred the way with their weapons of death. And as he sat there he saw many ships come that way. He knew them well, those ships of the Carian pirates that he had often fought against in Oenopion's service with his giant strength; and the pirates knew him too, and cried: " It is Orion." But he beckoned to them to land, and, as they came near, told them that the king's enemies were now his friends and they need fear nothing. Then they left their ships and came, bringing with them leathern bags full of wine pressed from stolen Chian grapes, and sat down beside their ancient foeman. As he told his woes they gave him to drink, and, oft as he wished them to fill the cup that fired his veins, they filled it, till sense and memory reeled and he lay stretched upon the sands in a drunken sleep. Thereupon the pirates rejoiced and sent up a mighty shout, "Our enemy is fallen, is fallen."

But the knowing ones said : "We must not leave him thus, for, when the fumes of the wine are gone, he may repent him and turn to the king's service and be our foe once more." So they put irons in a fire they made beside the shore, and when they were red hot they thrust them into the sleeping giant's eyes, and made haste back to their ships, not daring to look behind them. Orion awoke with the burning pain and staggered to his feet. He knew that an enemy had done this, but he could not see him. He heard the shouts, the laughter, the scorn of his boon companions of an hour ago, and in his impotent rage dashed after them into the sea, hurling great stones in the direction of their voices. Then the pirates made sail and hastened away, and Orion went back to the shore and lay there groaning in bitter agony.

All the glorious summer afternoon he tossed to and fro in helpless rage and pain, and when the sun went down and the stars of heaven came forth he knew it by the evening breezes that fanned his throbbing brow and the gentle dews that fell like balm upon his sightless eyes. The morning found him still awake but quieter, a weary, suffering, broken-hearted man ; for the many-voiced birds began their songs, the sweet scents of fresh opening flowers were wafted towards him, and he felt the beams of the sun as he rose above the dark cliffs of Asia. He knew the world was full of beauty and of glory, but not for him, and the tears of the strong man who had never wept before flowed from the aching eyeballs, as he thought of all that he had lost and would never see again. Then came the fierce noontide heat, and the tired giant's head began to droop like the flowers in the open meadow, while fitful dreams passed through his brain, dreams of the old loveliness of by-gone happy days, of green mother earth and restless tossing sunlit sea and the great blue dome of heaven, and, ever and anon, he would awake to a sense of his misery and cry, " O wretched man that I am," or he would pray to One he knew not, " My sight, my lost sight ; oh, give me back my sight."

So it circled round to night again, a calm, peaceful night, when all the noises of the day were hushed, and nothing broke the solemn stillness but the gentle ripple of the waves upon the beach. Nothing else ? Yes, there was something, Orion thought, for what his eyes had lost his ears had partly gained. He seemed to hear a far distant sound as of a heavy body falling every now and then in even time. And as he hearkened it grew more and more plain to his ears, till at last he said to himself, " It is the great hammer of Vulcan's forge at Lemnos." Then he remembered looking out at night over a long, clear stretch of sea away to the northward where Lemnos lay, and seeing the great pillar of smoke which arose from it up into the clear air, and the flames that glared at the base of the pillar, or shot their red light through its gloom, and when the night was dark were the only objects visible. He could not see the flames, but he could hear the hammer rise and fall, and the sound told him that the fire was there, though to him all was darkness. A joyful hope filled Orion's breast, for he thought that he who could make the brightness of day reign in night's gloom might also give back the light that had been stolen from his eyes and the joy of which his life had been robbed. Then he arose, saying, " I am going to the light," and cast himself into the sea.

Away through the quiet waters he went, wading at first till bottom failed him, and then swimming arm over arm in eager haste and with all his giant might. No voice was present to cheer the lonely traveller on his long sea-way, no sight of nearing land to fill his heart with hope ; nothing but the distant clang of the hammer on the great anvil and the knowledge that where the sound was, there the fire was to be found. Again and again he stopped to listen lest he should lose his course. At last his feet touch the sand. He is on land again ; but a strange misgiving fills his heart, for still, though nearer than it was, the sound that has led him is far away. Yet he hears voices joining in song and the music of well played instruments and a tinkling noise as of revellers whose golden ornaments jingle in the dance. And they call one to another, or it may be to him, to come to woody Lesbos, the home of mirth and happiness, the isle of music and of song. O poor Orion, it is not this you sought. A sorry figure the blind swimmer would make among these richly dressed, perfumed and laurel-crowned lovers of pleasure. He is almost tempted to rush in upon their revels and take revenge on them for the misery that, with-out knowing it, they mock so cruelly. But there is a lull in the music that lets the ring of the hammer sound out loud and clear, and it falls upon his ear like a voice crying " Come." His harsh, bitter laugh that had startled the dancers for a moment is changed to the voice of prayer as he hastens from the isle, and, spurning its shore from his eager feet, rises again upon the buoyant waves.

The Lesbian music is heard no more—nothing but the splash of the giant's great arms cleaving the waters on his onward course, and, keeping time with his strokes, the dis-tant hammer's clang. But the swimmer's strokes are telling now. He need not stop to listen for Vulcan's heavy blows upon the anvil. Nearer and nearer they seem to be, till at length Orion cannot hear his own motions, can hear nothing but the sound that rings in his ear, " Come, come, come !" So he comes to the shore of Lemnos, bruising himself as he lands on many a sharp piece of rock, and, guided still by the sound that fills all the air, staggers into the great forge that the Cyclops, giants like himself, had built in olden days for the King of Fire. Dripping with water from the sea, ragged and bruised and bleeding as he is, Vulcan takes the giant by the hand and sets him down beside the great furnace. Its generous warmth dries the soaking garments and gives back vigour to the benumbed limbs, and, for a moment, its glorious brightness tempts Orion to cry, " I see." But darkness reigns again ; he has felt but a glow after all and has seen no man. So he kneels him down and prays : " O Vulcan, lord of fire, give me back my sight again and I am your servant, your willing, grateful slave forever." But Vulcan, sad at heart and full of pity, answers : " That may not be, for I am no maker of light. The light that is given me from a higher source I use and spread abroad amid the darkness. With it I kindle the cheerful fire that gladdens man's heart and forge the weapons wherewith he may fight the powers of evil and the tools that aid him in every work that is good. But to give light to darkened eyes is only in the power of Him that gave the light to me."

Thus Orion's cup of hope was dashed to the ground. He forgot fhe genial warmth of the fire and Vulcan's kindly greeting and the smiths that left their toil to throng around him with generous words of welcome. " Was it for this," he cried, "that I left my home and braved the perils of the sea? You have deceived me, Father Vulcan, you and your blaze of light and the great hammer whose blows guided me to my disappointment. For me there is no hope. I will go back to be a terror and a curse among men, and fall at last upon Oenopion's spears." But Vulcan soothed the angry giant, saying: "Friend, I have done you no wrong in telling you what I cannot do; but I will not leave you thus. Are you willing to do more, to brave more, to suffer more, that you may gain your sight?" And Orion said, "There is nothing I will not do that I may get it back again." Then Vulcan cried, "Send me Kedalion;" and they brought a little lad, soft-voiced and gentle, with fair hair that streamed down upon his shoulders, and eyes blue as the summer's sky, and a face like those of the angels in heaven. So Vulcan took the boy and set him on Orion's knee, saying, "Behold your guide." Then Orion put forth his hand and touched him, but when he felt the long silken curls and the delicate form of the gentle lad, he was offended and asked if they meant to mock him by giving him such a guide. "Only trust him," answered Vulcan kindly, "and he will bring you to the Gates of Day, where He dwells, who can give light to your blind eyes." And the boy himself put his tender arms about the giant's neck and kissed him, whispering in his ear, "Only trust me and I will guide you safely, as I have often led others before." Orion's rough heart was touched. Half doubting and fearing, yet ashamed that it was so, and longing for the light, he placed the little guide upon his mighty shoulder, saying, "I trust you;" and away from the forge they went, Orion stepping forth with giant strides and Kedalion guiding with his clear blue eye.

What a journey that was for these two travellers, away
again through the deep sea to the Trojan shore, through the
many kingdoms of Asia Minor and the land of Ararat, past
the great empire of Persia and the nations of India, and
beyond the very world's end, where the silk-weaving Seres
dwelt! What sandy deserts they traversed, what mountain
ranges they toiled over, what rivers they forded, what seas
they swam! So eager at times was Orion, that, after a long
day's march when the night fell, he would not rest but still
press on, for night and day were all the same to his poor
eyes out of which the light had gone. And again, when the
long, weary road had tired even him, he would lie down in
field or jungle, by the roadside or on the shore, glad to
snatch a moment's sleep and dream some happy dream of
the bright day, while little Kedalion kept watch beside him.
There were many trials and sufferings for the giant and his
guide all along the way ; for wicked men, and men that called
themselves wise, and great giants like Orion himself, mocked
him and laughed at the gentle child upon his shoulder.
Even by force they tried to turn the blind man back and
take away his guide. Sweet voices, too, like those of the
sirens that lured the sailor to his death among the rocks in
the western sea, sounded often in Orion's ears, till he prayed
Kedalion to stop and listen to the heavenly music. But
Kedalion only bent over and placed his rosy lips close to the
ear that was nearest the sound, and whispered " Will you
have your sight again ?" Then Orion would press his
hands on either side of his head and heave a deep sigh and
run forward a long space till the music had died away. So
on they went, these two, to find the Gates of Day.

    At last they came to a place where it was very dark, so
dark that the cheery little guide said : " I cannot see to go

farther ; here we must rest, but light cometh in the morning." Orion laid the boy gently in his arms and, as he sat upon the ground, pressed him lovingly to his breast, for the darkness made his wounded eyeballs to ache again and a great sorrow filled his heart, and the child was his only comforter. All the long dark night Orion sat and waited, and, for the first time since they left Vulcan's forge at Lemnos, the little guide slept peacefully in his embrace. Then the night mist lifted and the black clouds rolled away. Kedalion awoke with a joyful cry : " Orion, Orion, I see the Gates of Day, the golden gates in the great wall of rubies and sapphires !" Then Orion fell upon his knees and placed his hand upon the head of the boy, saying : " Kedalion, I trust you." And so he waited. Nor did he wait long, for soon the golden gates flew open and the bright sun came forth in his chariot of glory. His warm beams fell upon the giant's sightless eyeballs till they ached no more, and a voice came down from heaven, just such a gentle voice as that which had comforted him all the way, so that he almost thought it was Kedalion who spoke : " What wilt thou, Orion ?" The giant trembled like a little child, trembled with fear and with hope ; but the little guide, upon whom his hand was resting, was the giant now. He never shook, but bravely bore up his friend that he might not fall. Then, while the sobs came thick and fast to choke his voice and his tears flowed down like summer rain, the blind man cried : " Lord, that I may receive my sight." And the beams of the sun shot forth towards him like golden hands that came to bless, making a rainbow over the weeping eyes. " Receive thy sight," said the gentle voice, and with the word Orion lifted up his eyes and saw ; then fell upon his face and worshipped.

No tongue of man can tell what Orion saw then ; it is

hidden deep down in the heart. Old things were passed away; all things had become new. It was as if he had become a babe again and been born into a new and lovelier world. Earth and sea and sky and all that was in them seemed touched with the glory that shone from the Gates of Day, so that the humblest little flower beneath his feet was fairer to his sight than the brightest jewel of Oenopion's crown or even the very stars of heaven themselves had been in the olden days. He looked for Kedalion that he might share his joy, but he was nowhere to be seen, for his work was done ; but instead of the fair-haired child, a bird, and a true bird of Paradise this was, perched upon the shoulder he had left and there warbled such notes of gladness as put a new song into Orion's mouth—a full heart's song of praise. And as he sang, his face turned upwards to the light that healed him. He saw the Monarch of Day moving ever onwards in his course of blessing, and, lifting up his arms, he cried: " Lord, I have none but Thee ; I will follow Thee whithersoever Thou goest ; give me some place behind Thy chariot wheels." But a voice came from the sky : " Freely thou hast received ; freely give. Go thou and lead the blind and the lost back to the great Physician and to their Father's house."

So Orion went back again with a joyous heart, seeking for the blind and the lame and the lost. And when he found them he carried them in the great strong arms of his giant love over the sea and the river, the desert and the mountain, speaking all the way the brave words of cheer that little Kedalion had taught him when he was himself a poor blind man. Many a cold, sick, weary wanderer he warmed and fed and kindly tended at good Vulcan's Lemnian forge, and many a one that had need of healing he bore far off to the

Gates of Day and with them waited patiently till the beams of the Sun of Righteousness made them whole. Then, when his work was done, he was carried away up into the blue heavens he loved so well, to shine among the brightest stars in the nightly firmament and guide the helpless sailor across the trackless sea.

Perhaps you have found out already who the real Orion is, the great, strong man, whom God made with a giant will, mightier than that of the holy angels in heaven. In Eden's beautiful garden he lived, and talked there with the King of kings, who loved him and gave everything into his hand. But the giant lost faith in his God, and disobeyed Him, and was driven out of Paradise. Then came all the sins and blinded his mind and ruined his life, till it seemed scarce worth living, as some poor blind men tell us to-day. But God put a longing in man's heart to see again, to see Him and the beautiful world that is only beautiful in Him. And while he is longing to see God there comes to his ears the sound of the Sabbath bell, that tells of those who are happy, because they are ever singing God's praises and doing His work. He tears himself away, first from his hopeless gloom, and then from the worldly pleasures that would tempt him ; and, in the company of God's people, finds comfort and hope. But they cannot give him the light he needs : only a guide to bring him to the light. The child Kedalion is a little text to believe with all the heart, such as " They that seek me early shall find me " ; " He that cometh unto me I will in no wise cast out ; " " God so loved the world that He gave His only begotten Son, that whosoever believeth in Him should not perish but have everlasting life ; " " This is a faithful saying, and worthy of all acceptation, that Christ Jesus came into the world to save sinners." The giant carries the text-guide, not on his shoulder, like Orion, but in his heart, and with it he goes far away from the world, whether by night or by day, till he feels that God is very near. Then he kneels down to pray, and as he prays, confessing his sins and asking for his sight, the Holy Spirit comes and opens his mind to see the pardoning God, and fills his heart with the joy and gladness of a child whom his father loves.

Now the old things are passed away and all things are become new. The world is full of light and happiness because it is full of God. The Christian, who once was blind but who now sees, will follow the Sun of Righteousness, that came to him with healing under His wings, wherever he leads. But to do this he must do the work of God. So back into the world he goes to guide the weary wanderers in sinful paths to the light of the Father's countenance, to carry them in his heart in prayer before the throne of grace, and to tell the blind ones who cannot see God, how he, once blind like them, can behold Him more clearly than aught else in earth or heaven. And then, when his work is done, God takes him home, with them that are wise, to shine as the brightness of the firmament, and with them that turn many to righteousness, as the stars forever and ever.

The King who had Horse's Ears.

The King who had Horse's Ears.

" If we confess our sins, He is faithful and just to forgive us our sins, and to cleanse us from all unrighteousness."—I JOHN, i. 9.

The same story often appears in different parts of the world, and this teaches us that all nations of men, although now far apart, once dwelt so near to each other that they were able to carry away the same legends and traditions. Herodotus, the father of history, who lived more than four hundred years before the birth of Jesus Christ, and Strabo, a geographer who wrote about the time that our Saviour was born, both tell of an army that was saved from destruction by mice which came through the night and gnawed their enemies bowstrings, so that, when the battle began, the archers were not able to shoot. That same story is told to-day by the Muskogees of the Indian Territory and the Utes of Colorado in the United States, two wild Indian tribes. So the king who had horse's or ass's ears appears in the old world legends as Midas of Phrygia, in Asia Minor, and as Lavra of Ireland. It is the story of Lavra I am going to tell.

There were many kings in Ireland in the old days, and each of these had his little court and army, but there was generally one greater than the others who was called king of all Ireland. At the time I speak of, Lavra was king of all Ireland, and kept his royal court in the famous palace of Tara. He had not come to the throne without trouble, for he had enemies. But the kingdom was his by right, many friends

2

gathered about him, and, as he had a strong army and was himself a brave bold soldier, he soon put down his foes and began his glorious reign. On the day that he was crowned, he sent messengers all over the country to the courts of the kings and the castles of all the nobles, inviting the harpers who lived in them to come to the palace of Tara, where they should play before the king. And the messengers promised in Lavra's name that the harper who played the best should receive as his prize a harp and a wreath of pure gold. So fourteen days after the king was crowned the harpers came flocking to Tara, along all the royal roads, from north and south and west, followed by great crowds of noblemen on horseback and people on foot, who wished to hear them sing and play.

At the end of the great hall sat the king of all Ireland upon his throne, and on either side of him, on lower seats, were the other kings, while brave soldiers and great officers of state stood on guard around them. The harpers marched into the hall in a long procession, dressed in flowing robes, and behind every one of them was a boy in a green tunic who carried his master's harp. Then came the noblemen, all richly clad, and took their places on seats along the walls, while the people staid outside and listened to the sounds of music and song that floated through the open doors and windows. So many were the harpers that three days passed before all could get a hearing, although the king and his court met three times a day in the great hall to try their skill. On the morning of the fourth day all came together again, and many a harper thought that he was going to win the precious prize. But the king's mind was troubled and confused, for neither he nor those who sat with him could tell who was the best harper of them all.

While Lavra was wondering in his heart what he should

do, there arose a noise and a shout at the lower end of the hall, and the guards called out so that the king could hear them, " Make way, make way for the harpers !" Then up the aisle came two tall figures of noble bearing, that might have been princesses of royal blood, and stood before the king. They were both beautiful, but the light-haired, meek-eyed one in the long white robe with the golden girdle had the beauty of the day, and the other in crimson raiment, whose dark locks were crowned with richly scented blossoms, wore the beauty of the night. No one asked them whence they came, or why they came so late, but all gazed in wonder upon the strange new-comers, and waited for their voices and the sound of their harps. The king arose from his throne to greet them and give a kindly welcome, and then the one in the white robe began to play.

As she struck the first few chords, the old, old harpers who had learned to play before the king's father was a baby in his cradle, bent forward their hoary heads to listen, for such a skilful easy touch they had never seen, such full rich, melting sounds they had never heard before. And when she lifted up her lovely head and sang, without casting a single glance at the harp strings that her fingers knew so well, the nobles and musicians held their very breath for fear that even a passing sigh should mar the heavenly music. Her song was of peace and purity, of goodness and truth and love ; and now the tones were strong and brave and clear like the silver trumpet that calls to a holy war, and now they were soft and gentle and low like the pleadings of a lady mother with her only child. Had you been there then you would have seen a strange sight. The musician's dark companion hid her face that was pale with envy and lined with angry thoughts behind the tapestry hangings of the hall ; the

nobles and soldiers withdrew their gloves of mail from their
sword hilts and clasped their hands before their breasts as if
in prayer ; and as the king listened eagerly, his head bent
forward and his cheek resting in his open palm, the tears, all
unnoticed by him or by any other, came trickling down upon
his royal beard. All the morning the sweet song lasted
though it seemed but a single hour, and when at last it
ended in a glorious burst of praise to the blessed God who
only is the true and the beautiful and the good, then all the
harpers, old and young, lifted up their voices as one man
and said : " Not unto us, not unto us, but unto her, O king,
let the prize be given."

Now she of the crimson robe came out from behind the
curtains, and with her sweetest smile and most appealing
glance knelt before Lavra saying, "Surely the good king
will hear me also." The king's heart was won by her looks
and words, for her fair companion had never once called
him good; and he was ashamed of the tear drops that he saw
upon his beard ; and, now that the music had ceased, he
began to feel hungry like common men, so he said, " We
will go and dine, and afterwards this lady shall have her
turn to try for the prize." Then they all marched away to
the great dining hall, and the dark musician ate and drank
beside the king, while the harper of the morning went out
among the common people and played and sang for them
and for many of the other harpers who came to listen such
sweet simple music and words as the people love.

When the feast was nearly ended and Lavra and his
nobles had almost forgotten what they had heard in the
morning, the rival musician arose and began to play. She
too knew well how to tune her harp and voice as she sang
of pleasure and rest, telling of cloudless skies and summer

days, of beautiful women and handsome men, of soothing sounds and sweet perfumes, of glittering jewels and great kings' palaces. Lavra and his courtiers yielded to the enchantment of the hour, and, half waking, half sleeping, dreamed they dwelt in lovely fairyland. Then came from the harp a sound of beating drums and ringing clarions, of marching men and banners flapping in the breeze, till all aroused themselves and grasped their swords. And now she sang of the fight begun, of gallant deeds of arms, of glorious victory, while the wondrous harp kept time with wild sounds that told the soldier of the rushing charge of horse and the steady tramp of footmen, the battle shout, the clashing of mingled weapons, and the very groans of dying warriors. But with all this there was no word of truth or goodness or love. Only when she ended her song with the homeward march of the victorious army, she praised King Lavra as man had never been praised before, calling him the greatest and wisest, the bravest and best of men, the mightiest monarch in all the world. Then the lesser kings and all the nobles drew their swords and waved them in the air crying " Long live Lavra, our king."

Back went the company to the great hall of Tara once more, and Lavra took the golden wreath and put it upon the dark singer's brow and placed the golden harp in her hand, and proclaimed her with his royal voice the chief of all the harpers of Ireland. Then the nobles shouted again, but the harpers looked black and had not a word to say, and the murmuring of the people without was like the hollow voice of the wind over the troubled sea. Up the aisle came the white-robed harper, looking so fresh and fair, so gentle and kindly, and yet withal so strong and brave, that the king's heart misgave him as he looked at her, and her rival turned away from her steady gaze. And she said, "O king, you have done yourself and your kingdom more harm than you have done me. When the great bell of Tara tolls the hour of midnight you will know who it was deserved the prize." Then she called to her dark companion, who sat beside the king, "Come, for your work is done;" and the proud, triumphant singer was forced to leave her seat and follow her down the aisle and out of the great gateway of the palace, till the two disappeared in the throng, and none could tell where they had gone, just as none knew whence they came.

The princes and nobles, the harpers and the people, went away to their homes, talking all the way ot the strange things they had seen and the wondrous music they had heard. . Only the king's own harper Craftine remained, together with the servants and guards of the palace. Lavra was tired after his four days' work of listening to many harps, and above all with the excitement of that last day, so he went early to rest and ordered faithful soldiers to guard the door of his bedchamber lest the fair singer he had rejected should try to do him harm through the night. At midnight he awoke and heard the single peal of the bell struck by the watchman in the tower to let weary watchers know that half the night was gone. Before its sound had died away the room was filled with light, and Lavra, sitting up, tried to call to his guard, but could not, for his lips were sealed. In the midst of the light the fair harper seemed to float before his eyes. As he gazed in terror upon the vision she said : " King Lavra, you have shown this day that your soul is that of a brute and not that of a man. As your soul is, so your ears shall be." And then she vanished and the light died away.

Lavra regained his voice and was about to call his guards, but, happily for him, before he did so he lifted his hand to his head, and, oh, horror ! he felt the long, hairy ears of a horse where his own shapely ones had been. He was over-whelmed with rage and shame, but what could he do ! He arose and fastened his door from within, that none might enter. Then, tearing down the hangings of his bed, he wound a long piece of tapestry round and round his head and these hideous ears till nothing could be seen of his new deformity. Soon as morning dawned, the king called his servants and sent them to find the most skilful worker in cloth in all his kingdom. The man was roused from his slumbers and brought to the king's bedchamber with all his stuff and working tools. Lavra ordered him then and there to make for him of the most costly material a tall ornamental cap such as those worn by great kings in far off eastern lands, which he, as the greatest of all kings, might wear, and over which he might place his kingly crown. So the terrified tradesman, little dreaming what the cap was for, set to work with all his might, and before it was time for Lavra to meet his nobles and to judge the people in the great hall of Tara, the cap was finished, and the poor man was sent away with a rich reward.

The nobles and the people who had come to get justice were astonished to see their king appear in their presence with this strange tall headdress, for Lavra used to sit among them with no other covering for his head than his long yellow hair encircled with the golden crown. So Lavra, like many other people, old and young, had to tell a lie to hide his sin. He said that they had all acknowledged him to be the greatest king in the world, and it was not meet that he should wear nothing more upon his head than subject princes were allowed to carry. Therefore, he said, he wore this cap to mark his greatness and the honour they had put upon him. But all the people wondered greatly when they saw that the king never went without this cap or one like it in court or review, at home or abroad, by night or by day. Then at length the king's cap began to be the fashion. The princes wore caps not quite so tall, and the nobles wore them a little shorter than the princes, and in the end even the people hid their shock heads of hair under skull-caps of different forms and colours. So nobody in Ireland paid any more attention to the king's head-dress.

But nature will out in spite of all we can do, and so it was with the king. His yellow hair grew long and thick till it became a great burden for one who loved field sports and out-door life. Lavra longed for the old days when his barber came and polled him, and now he had gone full two years without a hair of his head being cut. The heat caused by the hair and the cap made his royal head ache till he could bear it no longer. He ordered the barber to be called, but gave secret commands to the captain of his guard that the moment the man left the king's chamber he was to be gagged and hurried off to execution. The unhappy barber came. He saw the horse's ears upon the king's bare head and wondered if it was to be his task to cut them off. When told to poll the royal head, he thought of the grand scandal he would be able to tell to his friends, and felt so proud of his knowledge of the secret that he longed to be away and make it known. But when his work was done and he stepped lightly out of the king's chamber, he was seized by the guard and, as he attempted to speak, a wooden bridle— was thrust into his mouth and made fast behind his ears. Thus he was led away to the courtyard, where the executioner's sword finished the deadly work, and the body of the poor headless barber was buried out of sight. His wife and children and friends came to Tara asking where he was, but the king told another lie and said he did not know. So sad grief and mourning came to one family of the land because of Lavra's sin.

It was not long before the king's head had to be polled again. So another barber was brought into the palace to do the work, but nobody ever saw him come out of the gates or heard of him more. And soon after, another barber disappeared, and then another, till at last there were none left in the kingdom. Then Lavra ordered that clever young men should be looked out to take the place of the barbers· They came on in their turn to cut the king's hair, and after that were never seen again. There was weeping and mourning for lost friends all over the land and great fear fell upon all the people. Some of the boldest who had lost sons and brothers and husbands went to the court and asked Lavra to grant them justice and punish the murderers of their friends, but the king only laughed savagely and said that if they would tell him who the guilty persons were, he would have them punished. But Lavra, with the tall cap over his pale face and sunken eyes, looked so stern and harsh and cruel and had such a guard of soldiers as fierce as himself all around him, that the poor people did not dare to tell him what they thought. For in their hearts they felt that the king knew all about the death of their friends.

One day the officers came to the hut of a poor widow who had an only son, and said to her, " Your son must come and be the king's barber." The poor widow burst into tears at once and cried, " Oh, if King Lavra knew that he is my only son and all my support and comfort in the world,

surely he would not take him away." But the officers said,
" Hush, woman ! and be proud that the king honors your
son so much as to let him touch his royal head." Then the
widow answered, " Let the king honour somebody else and
let me keep my boy, for nobody that goes into the palace
to cut the king's hair ever comes out again." The officers
paid no attention to her cries but dragged her son away from
her embrace and led him off to Tara, while the poor old
mother ran after them weeping and crying out and tearing
her gray hair. So she pushed her way through the sentries
at the gate; none of the servants of the palace dared to stop
her, for they thought that she was mad, and the Irish in
those days would not dream of hurting a mad person ; and
at last she ran up the stairway and kept up her loud weeping and wailing in the royal hall. The king came out in his
great cap to learn the cause of the uproar, looking very
gloomy and stern, but the widow fell down at his feet and
prayed with all her mother's love that he would spare her
only son. Lavra's heart was touched, for there was some
little good left in him, and he ordered the guards and servants to go away and leave him alone with the young man
and his mother. Then he said, " Do you know why none
of those who came to poll me ever went out alive ! It is
because dead men tell no tales. Now, if your son is to live
he must take a solemn vow never to breathe to you, his
mother, nor to any man, woman or child, a single word or
hint of what he shall see in my bed-chamber. If he does,
then you and he and all he tells the secret to must be put to
death. Are you willing that he should take the vow ?" And
the mother cried, thankfully, " O yes, my kind king, my
good king, anything to save his life." So the widow went
home comforted, and the young man trembled as Lavra

made him take the solemn vow and then led him into his bedchamber.

Late in the afternoon the boy came home, dressed in fine clothes the king had given him, and with a little purse full of gold as his wages, which he gave to his mother. But no gold could have made her heart so glad as the sight of her son safe and sound. Yet she noticed that he looked very sad and unlike his own lively, joyous self. He did not sing nor even talk as he used to do, but would sit silent and idle half the day in the chimney corner, with his head in his hand and a troubled look in his eyes. And at night he would toss upon his bed and moan and sometimes cry out in a fright, "Did I tell the secret?"; or he would groan aloud, "Oh the vow, the terrible vow!" At last the king's gold was all gone for food, and, as her son did not work, the poor widow saw that they must soon starve unless she could rouse him and make him go out to his daily toil. So she called in a priest, a very wise man, and told him how her son was pining away because of a great secret that lay heavily on his breast, a secret he had bound himself by a terrible vow to tell to no man, woman or child, even the nearest and the dearest. The wise man thought a while, and then he asked, "Did he promise not to tell the secret to the winds and the waves, to the cattle and the trees?" And the mother answered, "No, not to these, but only to no man or woman or child." Then the priest turned to the young man and said: "Rise and go to the wood of Tara. There you will find an old oak tree with a hollow trunk. Put your lips to the hole in the trunk and tell your secret where no man or woman or child can hear, and then come back and do your work as before." When he had given this good advice the wise man departed.

The young man arose and ran all the way to the wood, full of impatience to tell the secret that was eating his life away. He found the tree, and, taking a hurried look all around to see that no person was near, he put his lips to the hole and cast his arms about the rough old trunk, as if it were the body of a dear friend that he embraced. Then over and over again he whispered and whispered, louder and louder, till his heart felt relief, " King Lavra has horse's ears, King Lavra has horse's ears." Now the load was off his breast. He was his old self again. He rañ, he bounded, he leapt, the same glad, joyous youth he was before the dreadful secret had taken away his strength and vigour. No evil dreams disturbed his rest that night, and, in the morning he went away to his work again, singing like the lark that flies to meet the rising sun. So the mother's heart was glad, and she blessed the good priest who had given her wise counsel.

You remember Craftine, the king's harper. Every day he played and sang to Lavra, and his music was good. But one morning Lavra had a sullen fit, and when Craftine played to him he said : " Take away that wretched harp. Its sounds are not fit to be heard in these halls where the lady harpers played so sweetly." Craftine thought within himself that their music had not done the king much good, but he óbeyed. But when he left Lavra's presence he was so angry because his harp was despised that he dashed it to the ground and broke it in many pieces. Afterwards he was sorry for what he had done, and, knowing that, when the king's sullen fit was over, he would send for him again, he only thought of how to mend the broken instrument. The harp-strings lay on the ground still perfect, but the wood of joy, as it was called, was so shattered that it could not be pieced together again, and, even if it could, the tone of the harp was gone for ever. Craftine must find a new wood of joy, all of one piece, without crack or flaw, of strange shape, and hard and dry, so that it should not shrink or rot. Away to the wood of Tara he hied him, and, searching long and diligently, came at last to the old hollow oak in whose hoary trunk the young barber's secret had been buried. Round about the very hole into which the widow's son had whispered his burden, Craftine saw the half circle of wood he needed. He called the carpenter to cut it from the dry and seasoned tree, and gave it into the hands of the wood carver, that he might polish it well and grave it with quaint device and fit it for the harp strings. All night he sat watching the carver at his work, and the sun had risen in the sky before the strings were fastened to the pegs ; and then, just as he began to tune his new-made harp, a royal messenger came, saying. '' The king is waiting for his harper.''

Craftine rose, put on his green mantle and carried the harp himself into the king's presence. Lavra was on his royal seat, surrounded by his nobles, and Craftine saw by his face that he was in a gracious mood. '' Come hither, Craftine,'' said the king, smiling, '' for we cannot do without your music, and in truth there is none like it, after all.'' So Craftine bowed his head in reverence and thankfulness to the king and then began to strike the cords. But as he struck, he trembled with awe and fear, and the nobles turned their heads aside, and Lavra moved uneasily upon his throne and hid his face in his hands. For the harp was like a sweetly mocking human voice, and, now like a chime of bells, now like a grand cathedral chant, it kept repeating these few truthful words : '' King Lavra has horse's ears, King Lavra has horse's ears, King Lavra has horse's ears.'' Craftine used all hisp owers. He tried to sing that he might drown the voice of the harp, but whether he would or no, he could only echo its painful

words : " Lavra has horse's ears." All the time the king's
face was working. Rage and indifference and smile of contempt came and went upon it, with terror and grief and the
sad look of rest that comes when the worst of sorrow is known.
A brave soldier who loved the king, spite of all his faults,
drew his sword and said : "Shall I sunder the cords, shall I
slay the man that unite to speak foul wrong of my king?"
Then the king rose quickly, motioned with his hand to put
back the sword, and with a great voice, that could be heard
far beyond the hall, he thundered " No !"

While the nobles and officers wondered what was about to
happen, Lavra gave command to throw open the hall doors
and let the people in who were waiting for him to sit on his
throne of justice. When the hall was full, he turned to
Craftine and said, " Strike your harp again " ; and Craftine,
trembling, struck his harp, hoping for some better strain. But
the same mocking voice came from its cords, " King Lavra
has horse's ears !" " Why do yon always play the same
thing?" asked the king ; and the harper answered : " Have
mercy upon me, Sire ; for it is the harp that repeats it against
my will, and that with all my power I cannot make say
anything else." Then Lavra said : " Let all the people listen,
for this harp's voice is the voice of God against whom I have
sinned that comes to condemn me." He took off his royal
crown and laid it on the floor at his feet, saying " I am not
fit to wear a crown, for I have been the slayer of my people
and not their friend." Next he lifted the tall cap from his
head and cried, " See what a king you have ; mock him and
curse him, for he deserves it and more beside." But the
nobles and all the people lifted up their hands. and with one
voice they shouted, till the hall rang again with their shouts,
" Long live King Lavra, long live the king !" For when

Lavra raised the cap, meaning that they should see the hideous ears, they saw nothing but the long yellow hair of olden days that streamed down upon his shoulders. And as it seemed to them that they had got back again the kindly, simple-hearted monarch they had loved, they shouted once more " Long live King Lavra, long live our king !"

Lavra wondered with great astonishment till his eye rested upon a shield of polished steel which hung near by, and there, reflected from its bright surface, he saw his kingly form just as it had been in the olden days ; for the cause of all his auguish and deceit and cruelty, the horrid ears were gone. So the king knelt down before all the people, and when they saw him kneeling, they knelt too, and he prayed a prayer that was full of heart-broken thankfulness to the great wonder-working God in heaven. And when it was ended, though the people knew not what it was all about, they were sure from the look of the king's face that it was true and good, and all together said " Amen." Then up through the press came the well-known figure of the white-robed harper, and bending low beside Lavra she picked up the golden crown and placed it on his royal head, and as she led him back to his throne, breathed not a word of reproach or blame, but only said, " God save the king !" which filled the hall with joyous shouts once more. After that she called Craftine and bade him tune his harp in unison with her own ; and they two played before the throne. It was strange to listen to Craftine's playing, for his truthful wood of joy had lost its mocking tone and dismal strain, and seemed to catch every note that fell from the white harper's fingers with so full and sweet a sound that it was hard to tell which was the diviner music. All the time the king sat thinking, thinking bitterly of the sad, sad past, till the harpers sang of the angels' joy in heaven over the sinner who repents of his wicked ways and comes back to truth and right again. Then Lavra arose and blessed his people in the name of the great forgiving God. Raising his hand to heaven he promised to make amends for all the evil he had done, and from that time forth to reign in truth and righteousness, the father and friend of his subjects, and the constant lover of all that is right and good.

Lavra kept his word. There was great joy and gladness in Tara, for the king, no longer shut up in his palace, was ever among the people, seeking out the families that had suffered by his cruel orders that he might do them all the good in his power, and caring for all the sick and poor and sad and erring, as if they were his own children. The white-robed harper had departed, unnoticed as she came ; but whenever an evil spirit troubled Lavra, he sent for Craftine to play before him. And Craftine's harp had so learned her song of truth and beauty and goodness that it filled the heart of the king, and drove the evil spirit far away. After a few years the wicked spirit came no more, but Craftine still kept on harping, and Lavra became wiser and better every day. Many people came to him to learn what had made his life so happy and good, and chief of all the advice he gave them, even when his yellow locks were white with age, was this : " Confess your fault and all will be well."

Like the Irish king, when we are setting out on life's journey, we gather around us our harpers. They are the voices we listen to, the books we read, the examples that are set before us. Among them come temptations to evil, and lessons of truth and goodness. The white-robed harper is the Book of books, the Word of God, that sings divine

songs in our ears such as the voice of man never uttered, to lead us into the paths of peace and holiness.
When we will not hear that song, but prefer the music of
the world, then sin comes into our hearts and takes up its
lodging there. Pride and falsehood and suspicion and
malice and murderous thoughts follow each other, till our
conscience condemns us and our life becomes a sad,
dreary, wretched scene, painful to ourselves and hurtful to
others. But God does not leave us. He sends His good
angel to whisper better things, and when the time comes,
conscience, like the wood of joy, tells us of all our faults and
the ugliness of our moral nature. Then, if we are wise,
like King Lavra, we will confess our sins to God and ask
Him, who knows everything, to look into our hearts and
see all the evil that is there, and give us new hearts to love
and serve Him. If we believe that God so loved us, wicked
as we are, that He sent His Son to die for us, our evil conscience, like the horse's ears, will vanish away, and by His
grace we will be made strong to do that which is good,
to repair past wrong, and to be helpful to those among
whom God has placed us in the world. For when we confess our sins, God is faithful and just to forgive us our
sins and to cleanse us from all unrighteousness.

●

III.

The Beautiful House.

■

III.

The Beautiful House.

" Make to yourselves friends of the mammon of unrighteousness ; that when ye fail, they may receive you into everlasting habitations."—Luke xvi. 9.

Who has not heard of Egypt, that old, old land, and of its famous city Alexandria? It was in that city that the things happened which I am about to tell. Alexandria was looked upon as a new city by the native Egyptians, for while Memphis and Thebes were in the height of their pride and glory when Moses was born and before a word of the Bible had been written, it was only built by Alexander the Great little more than three hundred years before the Saviour of man came as a babe to the cradle of Bethlehem.

Many hundreds of years ago, when Alexandria was a Christian city, and before the Arabians with sword and fire entered it to kill and destroy and set up the false religion of their prophet Mahomet, there lived in that city a patriarch named John. This patriarch was a kind of archbishop, the chief of all the clergy in Egypt. But although he had been raised so high, he was not a proud or a vain man. He was like the Apostle John, his namesake, gentle, loving and kind, fond of little children, good to the poor, and caring very little what became of himself so long as he did God's work. One of his friends was the Bishop Troilus, who used to preach in Alexandria and teach the young men and visit the people in their homes. John loved Troilus because he was a good man and tried to serve God and be useful in the world. He was a wise man, too, and a scholar; this only could be said against him, he was too much in love with money. Troilus was á miser, and like many misers, he was so afraid thieves would take away his gold, that he either hid it in a safe place or carried it about with him.

One day Patriarch John and Bishop Troilus had their donkeys saddled and rode out of the city away to the sea shore. Riding along the sands they had very pleasant talks on the way about the beautiful works of God they saw all around them, and about their own little work for God in Alexandria. Troilus enjoyed the afternoon very much, and said to John how thankful they should be that they were not like the poor Christians in the West who were being killed or driven from their homes by savage enemies. Just then John looked forward and saw a great cloud of dust some distance off; and as he looked more closely, he saw that it was made by a large company of people coming towards them. So he and Troilus rode on quickly and came up to the company. What a sad sight it was ! There were hundreds of people there, but they looked like so many ghosts. Old grey haired men and women who could hardly hobble along even with the help of their sticks and crutches ; young men and women that should have been strong and fair, but that were so wasted with starvation as to be mere walking skeletons ; and little children crying piteously for bread or to be taken up into the arms of their poor fainting fathers and mothers : that was what John and Troilus saw.

A tall, dark-faced man in a long black robe came forward when he saw that John and Troilus were clergymen, and spoke to them in the Latin language, which they knew, although their own language was Greek. He told John that he had been the minister of many of these poor people, who

loved God and tried to walk in His ways. But armies of
wicked men had come into their country. They sacked the
towns and villages, killed many of the young men, and made
slaves of all whom they took prisoners. So he and his people left the town where they lived and set out for Egypt,
choosing rather to perish on the way than fall into the hands
of their cruel enemies. As they went onwards they were
joined by many others who were fleeing for the same cause,
until they became a great company of helpless, suffering
creatures. Some had fallen down by the way and died.
Old people and little children, and even some mothers and
fathers that had seemed strong and healthy, had been hastily
buried in the sands, that no ravenous beast or bird might
devour them, while the sad procession moved on. And now
here they were at last, so hungry no one could tell who had
not gone for days without food, their clothes all soiled and
torn, their shoes worn away, their flesh blistered with the
sun and aching with many sores made by the dust and
drifting sand, and so tired and weary that again and again
some of them had prayed their friends to let them lie down
and die. " My father," said the African bishop to Patriarch
John, " find some food, some clothes, some shelter, some
rest, for my poor flock and God will reward you."

John's heart was touched with what he heard and saw ;
for never before had he known such misery. Troilus, too,
was drawing his sleeve across his eyes in a suspicious way
and saying in his mind how thankful he ought to be. " If
they will come into the city," he said to John, " we will take
up a collection for them." But John waved his hand, as
Troilus thought too impatiently, and answered : " How dare
we ask these weary, starving creatures to go a step farther ?"
Then turning to the minister, he said : " Let them go aside

under the shade of these trees ; there they will find rest, and
water to quench their thirst in the meantime." So the people
lay down under the trees and tried to rest. " Brother
Troilus," said the patriarch, " we must do something for the
friends of Christ, and yet I have no money with me ; give me
thirty pieces of gold." Now thirty large pieces of gold was
a great sum, and to be asked for so much almost took away
the bishop's breath ; but as John was his chief he had to obey,
and count it out of his purse. John put the money into the
hands of the African minister, and, giving him his ass, told
told him to go with Troilus into the city and buy food enough
for the people, while Troilus should call together all the
presbyters and deacons and get them to provide shelter and
clothing, baths and medicines and all else that the persecuted friends of Christ might need. So away they went into
Alexandria, the minister's heart full of deepest joy and
gratitude, that of Troilus heavy and sad.

Patriarch John staid with the people under the trees. He
saw an old man who had lost his headdress and whose head
was quite bald, so that he was ashamed of himself. To him
he went up, called him father, and put his own hat upon his
head. A youth who was supporting his old mother had no
shoes. There were deep cuts in his feet, and the sand got
into them and made them so painful that he could hardly
keep down a groan as he limped along. John took water
from the well, washed the wounded feet and put his own
sandals upon them. Then he saw a poor wan mother,
lightly clad, with a baby at her breast, looking for some
place to lie down while the baby slept. So the kind patriarch took off his cloak, laid it on the ground, and led the
weary woman to this couch as respectfully as if she had
been a noble lady. After that he walked about with bare

head and feet, finding comfortable places for the old, soothing
the fretful children, carrying water to the thirsty, washing
the cuts and sores of the wounded and binding them up with
pieces of his own clothes, all the time speaking kindly words
to all and telling them of the food and other good things
that were coming. Soon the minister came with a great
train of men and animals carrying bread and figs and many
things beside. What a sight it was to see these hungry
people eat, and above all to see how strong and glad they
seemed after a few mouthfuls had put new life into them !
Then after they had eaten and drunk, and the very old and
the sick and the very young had been put on the animals
and in the baskets that had brought the food, they started
for the city. And all the way John walked beside a sick
old grandmother, holding her up on his ass, looking, for all
his bare head and feet and tattered clothes, as noble and
grand as he was true and good. So they came to Alexandria, where the presbyters and deacons, and many good
people whose hearts God had touched, met them and carried
them away to restful, happy homes. But the patriarch was
so busy looking after the comfort of everybody that he did
not notice, what surprised all the presbyters and deacons,
Bishop Troilus was not there.

Now Troilus had done all that John had commanded.
He had helped the African bishop to buy food for his
starving people, and had called together the presbyters and
deacons of the Church that they might hear the sad story
and do all in their power to help the sufferers. He did not
tell the bishop that the large gold pieces which he paid to
the merchants for food came out of his purse, for he did not
want the bishop's thanks. Nor when he assembled the officers of the Church did he let them know how he, Troilus,

had advanced so great a sum of money for the relief of the
fugitives, for he was not a vain man eager to have much
made of his good deeds. But all the time he was thinking
how long it would be before the great gap in his money-bag
would be filled. Then he blamed John in his heart, because
John had so much more to live upon and do good with than
he, a poor bishop. It was all very well for a rich patriarch
to distribute thirty pieces of gold as if he were a king, but for
one who had to toil for his daily bread it was quite another
matter. Besides, why should he bear the burden of all these
people when he was only one man out of many thousands of
Christians in Alexandria, all of whom were bound to help
their suffering brethren. The right thing would have been
what he had advised—a collection. Then the expense
would have been spread over the whole Church, and a piece
of silver from every member of the Church would have
amounted to far more than his thirty pieces of gold. Also,
this would have taught the people the duty of giving—a
lesson they very much needed, in spite of all his earnest
preaching.

Along with these regretful thoughts a great fear came upon
Troilus that John might not be satisfied with the thirty
pieces, but, finding he was rich enough to give so much,
might ask for more. So he hastened home to leave the rest
of his money in a safe place before he went back to meet the
patriarch. In the strong box under his bed he put the gold
pieces, and as he counted them out, thirty short of what he
numbered in the morning, the full extent of his loss dawned
upon his mind and his heart became heavy as lead. He
had hardly closed the box and pushed it back into its place
when a cold chill ran through all his body ; the blood rushed
to his head ; for a moment his brain seemed to be on fire ;

and then he fell in a faint upon the floor and knew nothing. His wife came running in, full of fear when she heard the fall, and knelt beside him, thinking he was dead. She raised his head while servants brought wine and water to restore him. They bathed his forehead with the water, poured some wine into his lips, and rubbed his hands and feet, till at last he came to himself and, opening his eyes, said: " I must go back to the patriarch and to the poor friends of Christ." But this his wife and the neighbours who had come in would not let him do. He had been working too hard, he had exposed himself to the heat of the sun, he had been trying his brain with too much study ; so they said he must rest, and they would let John know why he could not go back to him that day. But as they all promised to tell the patriarch, and as everybody thought that some other body would be sure to do so, John never heard that the bishop whom he loved was sick.

Troilus was laid upon his couch, and, having nothing to do, began again to think of his lost gold. His attentive wife brought him the delicacies that sick people like, but the bishop would not touch them. He muttered some nonsense about being too poor to eat such food, and cautioned his wife to be careful in her household expenses, for he was nearly a ruined man. And she was just a little offended at receiving such advice, for she was a bishop's daughter and prided herself upon knowing how to make a little go a long way. But she thought that her husband's head had been hurt by a sunstroke perhaps, or, it might be, by his fall when he fainted. So she left him in hopes that he would be better after a quiet sleep. Troilus did not sleep. All night he tossed upon his bed thinking of his gold. He went over his old reasonings as to how the needed money should have

been raised, till he worked himself into a frame of what he
called righteous indignation, and felt that in all Alexandria
there was not a more abused man.   He forgot his Scripture-
reading, without which he had never opened or closed the
day since he gave himself to the work of God, and, worse
than all, he forgot to pray.   If he had prayed, his prayer
would not have been " Our Father," but " Give me back
my thirty pieces of gold."

In the morning he was very ill.   He could take no food,
and this, with his want of sleep and painful thoughts, made
him so pale and haggard and weak that he looked like an old,
old man.   His friends were in great grief.   A wise physician came, but with all his wisdom could not tell what was
the matter with the bishop, and Troilus would not let him or
anybody else know his trouble.   Still the foolish man hugged
his sorrow, and the cry of his heart, which seemed to shed
tears of blood with every cry, was " my gold, my lost gold,
my thirty broad pieces of gold."   At last his mind and
body could stand the strain no longer.   Troilus fell into a
raging fever.   In his fever he was like a raving madman.
Sometimes his look was wild and fierce like that of a savage
beast.   Then he would clutch the bedclothes as if he had
hold of somebody's throat, crying out " Give me back my
money."   And again his face was full of terror as he seemed
to be holding back one who was advancing towards him, to
whom he called, " no more, not one farthing more !"   Now
he would sink back upon his pillow with such a sad pitiful
expression, almost sobbing, " Oh John, John, why did you
rob your poor bishop?" ; or he would go on for hours muttering like some feeble childish idiot "my thirty pieces of
gold."

Troilus' wife wondered very much that the patriarch did

did not come to see her husband. But in truth nobody had told him that Troilus was ill, and, although he missed his bishop, he was so much taken up with the fugitives that he quite forgot to ask the cause of his absence from the church. So after Troilus had been three days in bed she went to see John. She told him how very sick he was, of his raving in his fever, how not even the wise physician could tell what was the cause of his sickness, and that he was always talking about some lost money. John was very sorry, because he loved Troilus. He left his work and went to see him, but Troilus did not know who he was. The good patriarch knelt down and prayed that God would heal his friend, but all the time that he prayed it shocked him to hear the sick man call out, " Oh my gold, my gold, my lost gold !" Then John knew what was the matter with Troilus. So he said to his wife " My poor brother gave me thirty pieces of gold, the day that the persecuted friends of Christ came to the city, to buy them bread, and now he is afraid that without this money you and your children will be left to starve. I will send you the pieces as soon as I return home, for I only meant to borrow them for a short time, and you must find some way of letting him know that his gold is not lost." So the patriarch went home very sad in his heart, not so much because Troilus was sick, as because his sickness was a poisonous plant springing from the love of money, which is the root of all evil.

A few minutes later a servant came with a bag of money and handed it to the bishop's wife. Troilus was lying back upon his pillow murmuring " My thirty pieces of gold, my thirty pieces of gold." As he was quiet and his bed was undisturbed, his wife took the coins out of the bag and laid them one by one upon the coverlet just above his knees.

Soon Troilus sat up and was beginning to tear his hair in his grief and madness, when his eye fell upon the gold. He looked at it with fixed gaze for a moment, and then, with a strange foolish chuckle, like that of a crazy person who sees something which pleases him, he stretched out his hand and touched the money. The touch thrilled him, as if the gold were a living thing. He picked up the pieces one after another and piled them up in his other hand. Then he spread them out again upon the bed and counted them. Yes, they were all there : thirty pieces of gold, broad pieces, bright and shining. His wife watched him through the door and thanked God in her heart as she saw how calm and reasonable he became. When Troilus was tired of looking at his gold and counting it, he laid it under his pillow just beneath his head, and then sank into a quiet refreshing sleep, the first that had visited his eyes since his sickness began.

He awoke in his right mind. The past three days he had no remembrance of, except as a troubled dream. His fever had almost left him, and, although faint and weak, he was very happy because he could put his hand under the pillow and feel that his money was there. No one had told him where it came from, but he knew that it was the patriarch who had returned it as if it were a loan, and now he had no thoughts too kind and good for the man whom he had judged so harshly a little before. He did not complain of the food that his glad wife brought him, but ate and drank heartily, and even asked for his children that they might receive their father's blessing. There was joy in the bishop's house that night, and among his friends and neighbours, as he fell into the easy restful sleep of returning health. So Troilus slept until the morning dawned, and then, just as

the busy round of daily life began outside his closely cur-
tained windows in the streets of the city, it called him into
that strange state between sleeping and waking when visions
pass through men's minds, and Troilus dreamed a dream.

He was walking, or floating, for he could hardly tell which,
in a new country of rare beauty. Far as the eye could
reach it was one great garden, whose grassy slopes were
covered with unnumbered shrubs and flowers of delicious
perfume and gorgeous colouring. Fountains of purest water
shot up into the air and broke into delicate spray which
watered the green sward, or swelled the little rills that flowed
onwards in many a tiny cataract to join the great river below.
And the great river itself poured its mighty tide over
golden sands with a grand yet joyous rythmic motion that
sounded as if ten thousand human voices were singing
psalms to God. Then Troilus knew, though he could never
afterwards explain it, what is meant by the voice of many
waters. There were giant trees upon the river's banks, laden
with all manner of fruits, such as neither Egypt nor the land
of Palestine had ever known, and on their ever-green branches
perched and sang birds of the richest feathering and most
melodious voice. The dwellers in this Paradise were clad in
robes of dazzling whiteness, and on every brow there shone
a royal crown of gold and gems. Nor was there lack of
habitations meet for these princely inhabitants. On every side
rose palaces embowered in leafy shades, surrounded by grassy
lawns and approached by ancient avenues. Troilus felt
ashamed of himself in his humble garb and mean appearance
amid such scenes of beauty and splendour. He would fain
have shrunk away into some quiet corner, but something
seemed to push him forward till he came in front of a palace
which the workmen were just finishing. It was of marble,

white and polished, grander in its proportions than the most
famous Grecian temple.   Its pillars were of great transparent
stones of changing colours, the names of which he did not
know, and its pinnacles of solid gold.   A man stood by his
side and, pointing to the great portico that formed the
entrance to the palace, said simply "Look !"   Then Troilus
looked upwards and saw a ladder set against the portico, and
on the ladder an angel, for so he seemed, with chisel and
mallet in his hand.   The angel was engraving an inscription
over the door ; and when he had ended his work and stood
aside to look at it, Troilus read the words : " The everlasting
mansion and resting place of Bishop Troilus." No sooner
had the bishop read these welcome words than he sprang
forward and, with a great shout of joy, awoke.

The sick man was sorry that he had awakened so soon
out of sleep, yet he thanked God for such a vision, and
prayed that he might dream it again.   Yet before he dozed
off into a second sleep he put his hand beneath his
pillow and felt his gold, to be sure that it was there.
Once more the sights and sounds of this world faded
away from eye and ear, and he found himself anew in
the garden country of many mansions.   Everything seemed
even more beautiful than when first the heavenly scene
gladdened the eye of his spirit, so that he longed to bring all
his friends to this new land, and with them live there forever.   But he was most anxious to see his own mansion, which
before had appeared so fair and stately.   With quick steps
he hastened over the flower-sprinkled turf and up the avenue
of majestic cedars, till he stood opposite the well-known
portico.   And now it seemed as if the sun were shining down
upon the palace with the warm, mellow light of evening, for
it was ten fold more glorious than before, so dazzlingly white

were its marble walls, so radiant its glassy pillars of varied hues, so bright and shining its roof and pinnacles of burnished gold. Lightly he pressed on to the broad steps which led to the portico, eager to take possession of the mansion which had been built for him, and that bore his very name and office upon its arched doorway; when the grave stranger, who had told him to look before, placed his hand upon his arm and again said: "Look!" So Troilus, a little impatient at being checked, and expecting to see nothing that had not met his view when last he turned his eyes to the portal, gave a somewhat angry glance upwards. The ladder and the angel were still there, and this seemed strange to him because the sculptor's work had been finished, the inscription completed at his first visit. "Look," again said the speaker, and Troilus looked more attentively, and, as he looked, a sad change came over his heart, and burning blushes glowed upon cheek and brow. With mallet and chisel the old inscription had been struck off from the arch. A new one, just finished, had taken its place, and Troilus read it in grief and pain: "The everlasting mansion and resting place of John the Patriarch, which he bought from Bishop Troilus for thirty pieces of gold." The Bishop awoke the second time, and, when his wife came to smooth his pillows and to learn how he had he passed the night, she saw that he had been weeping bitterly.

Troilus had fallen from the heights of bliss almost to the brink of the gulf of despair. He had seen the land of promise in all its beauty, but there was no place in it for him. Worse than all, his heavenly mansion had passed into the hands of another, and all because of his own blind folly and sinful love of earthly things. What was the value of these wretched thirty pieces of gold for which he had bartered his everlasting dwelling-place! They were not enough

4

to gild a single pinnacle of the house that once bore his name. So the bishop came to his better self, and with a humble, penitent heart he prayed to the great builder of all things, who is God, that he would pardon all his sins for the sake of that Blessed Saviour who said, "In my Father's house are many mansions—I go to prepare a place for you." Then he called his wife and told her of all his faults and the wonderful dreams that God had sent to teach him heavenly wisdom. He gave her the thirty pieces and bade her take thirty pieces more from the strong box beneath his couch and carry them all to John, that the good Patriarch might spend them upon the poor friends of Christ. John was glad when the bishop's wife came with the gold, because in that gold he saw how great were the riches that God had poured into the heart of Troilus. What a meeting it was when the Patriarch came to visit his bishop. He had loved Troilus well before, but now that his life was raised above earthly things and wholly given to God, he loved him with tenfold affection. With one mind and heart they went about their Master's work henceforth, so that no poor friend of Christ could tell which of them he loved the most, so perfectly had each received the spirit of Him who "though He was rich, yet for our sakes became poor." Many happy dreams had Troilus after the busy labours of the day were done, and when at last his life's day ended and faithful friends stood round his dying bed, they heard the bishop's voice : "I see it, I see it ; it is real, it is true, it is no dream ! the everlasting mansion and resting place of the poor sinner Troilus." And so he passed away into the Paradise of God, the House of many mansions.

No gold can win heaven, for it is not with corruptible things such as silver and gold, but with the precious blood of Christ that all are saved. But no covetous man who is an idolater hath any inheritance in the Kingdom of Christ and of God. So the blood of Jesus Christ must wash away from our hearts the love of money and all earthly things, and His Holy Spirit must teach us to esteem them all but dross, as matters of little value, compared with the love of God. Then, if the love of God be in our hearts, we will love His people, His poor friends, His little ones. The dross will be useful in enabling us to relieve their wants, and thus show that our love is real and true. In this way we shall make friends of the unrighteous mammon. And when at last we stand before the great Redeemer, it will be in a very true sense these tokens of our faith and love that will receive us into everlasting habitations, for His gracious words will be, " Inasmuch as ye have done it unto one of the least of these, my brethren, ye have done it unto me. Come ye, blessed of my Father, inherit the Kingdom prepared for you from the foundation of the world." All may not have the thirty pieces of gold to give, but if they have the Christ-like heart, it will make any gift of great price in His eyes who said, " Whosoever shall give to drink unto one of these little ones a cup of cold water only in the name of a disciple, verily I say unto you he shall in no wise lose his reward."

IV.

The Indian Girl and the Flowers.

The Indian Girl and the Flowers.

" And now abideth faith, hope, charity, these three ; but the greatest of these is charity."—I. CORINTH. xiii. 13.

Once, so the story tells us, there were no flowers in North America. There were cones upon the pines and cedars and hemlocks, catkins on the birches, and reddish hanging tufts upon the maples that turned afterwards into winged seeds. The marsh grass also had its blossom, and so had the corn in the clearings, and the wild gooseberries and currants that grew in the rocky clefts. But there were no showy flowers, none of beautiful colour and sweet perfume, to make into a nosegay, or twine into wreaths for the heads of the Indian girls. In summer the earth was green with the grass and the foliage of the trees, and brown and grey with the tree trunks and the rocks and soil beneath ; and in winter all was white with the snow, except when the wind shook it down from the dark tops of the leafy evergreens, and made bare the grey leafless trunks of the hardwood trees. All the bright colour men saw was either in the skies above or in their reflection upon the earth. On a bright, clear morning, as the sun arose, there was a red light in the east, that changed after a while to a golden yellow. It fell upon the distant hills and gave them hazy purple tops, upon the rocks and made them glow like silver, upon the trees and gilded their greenery till it shone like a beetle's wing. Then the blue sky came in sight and at once found its reflection in the waters of lake and river, which before were as dark and gloomy as the forest shades. And at evening, when the sun was setting, it was even more glorious ; for the western sky and the woods and waters were all flooded with many hued waves of light, crimson and purple, yellow and azure, and light golden green, glowing up or fading away into each other till the darkness of night came on. Sometimes, too, through the day, when the light rain fell from fleecy clouds while the sun was shining, a rainbow would suddenly start from either horizon across the sky, and in its seven-tinted ribbon display all the colours at once.

In those days there was an Indian village on the shore of one of the Canadian lakes. It was placed at the end of a bay, long but shallow, in which the Indians in their canoes fished, or hunted the deer that their dogs had driven out of the woods. The people who lived there were quite contented with their lot, as their fathers had been before them. So long as the crop of Indian corn was good, as the sweet maple sap ran freely in the early spring, and as fish and deer were to be found in plenty, they were happy and cared for nothing else. They liked a clear sky and dry weather, because they felt these to be pleasant and comfortable, but the brightness of the sunset and the sunrise were nothing to them but signs of what the day or the morrow would be. They had never known what flowers were, and did not feel the want of them. Now and again, when they dressed themselves out in their holiday clothes of deer-skin and furs, and looked at their belts and collars of black and white beads, made out of the shells that once came from a distant shore, those who were fondest of show thought of the colours in the skies and longed for a moment to dip their finery in them. But the wish soon passed away as an impossible thing, and they went back to their black and white and green and brown as if there were no other colours in the wide world.

There was one, however, who thought differently. She was a little girl who had come into the village, nobody seemed to know how. Whether she had strayed there alone or had been left by some wandering tribe, or had been made prisoner in war, none were willing to tell if they knew. She lived in the house of an old chief, where there were some women and young men but no children beside herself. Because she was pale, and her neat deerskin dress was tanned very white, she had been called Owistok, the snow-bird, the winter visitor of the snowy north that loses its white coat when the spring comes in, and in its grey cloak and hood, with white breast and beak and feet, looks so like a demure little nun. Just as demure and pretty, but more quiet and gentle was the little bird's name-sake, Owistok. Girls were not much thought of in those old Indian days, but, perhaps, because she lived in the house of the old chief, and certainly because she was so wise and good, everybody had a kind word for the young foundling. She tried to be helpful to all, to the old women in their hard out-door work and household duties, to the young women with their babies, and to the children like herself in their play. She would sit with the fishermen and supply them with bait, would carry in her share of the corn harvest, boil down the maple sap into sugar, and be the first to welcome the hunters home. Even the dogs knew her, and when driven away by others, were always sure of a refuge and a bone in her company. But although she was so willing and so kind, she was not strong ; and many a time as the men and women looked after her, going away tired and weary from some good work beyond her strength, they would say : " Our little Owistok will fly away with the other snow-birds before another summer comes.

The Indian girl loved the sky, and she loved the earth most when the colours of the sky shone upon it. These colours were something real in her eyes, and she wanted them. Why did they only come for so short a time and then fade away ; all except the blue of the water, and that hardly lasted for more than a day? Sometimes, indeed, the lake remained beautiful all through the night, with the silver moonbeams glancing over its sapphire waves and the star points flickering on its surface. She was tempted to take some of its water up in her hand, to dip some up in a bowl of coarse earthenware, hoping to keep the blue near her. Alas! the blue faded away, and she saw nothing but the well-known colour of hand and bowl instead. Still she did not give up her confidence. There was blue somewhere if it was not in the water. She ran a mile along the shore to find the end of the rainbow arch, only to see it vanish from sight. She climbed a hill top early in the morning to bathe herself in the violet light, and paddled her canoe in the evening far into the sunset, in hopes that even one ray of glory might descend upon her, but all in vain. Yet still, though bitterly disappointed, she believed that the colours she saw were real and true. She could not name the colours nor describe them to anyone. She only knew that they were beautiful, that they did her good to look at them, and that she would be more happy if she had them somehow to herself.

Owistok was not selfish in her love of the colours. She wished to make the world more beautiful and the people in it happier by their means. She saw a young squaw standing in the rosy light of the morning, and noticed how lovely she looked. What would she not have given to make that passing loveliness stay ! She gathered sprigs of herbs and leafy twigs of many trees, and wove them into a garland, then hung the garland about a baby's neck. The fading sunlight shining down through the trees fell upon the different shades of green that she had woven, giving them such a brightness and newness of colour that the little child clutched the leaves as a coveted prize. Then Owistok cried like a baby herself, because the little fellow threw the garland away when he found it was made of nothing that he had not seen before. A canoe came round a point just then full into the glow of the western sky. The water was calm, and the canoe seemed to stand high out of it, and the two Indians who were paddling appeared to be giants, but such radiant heavenly giants, in a ship of gold with paddles of silver gently gliding over a crimson sea, that she ran to the beach to meet them, hoping to see visitors from another world. The canoe came in, a common, dirty log canoe, paddled by two of the commonest Indians in the village; and Owistok stood dumb with disappointment and holding her hands before her eyes for very shame. And when she came to herself she could not tell the men what she had seen far off and hoped to see near, because it would only make them unhappy to think they were so unlike her vision of beauty.

One day the girl ventured to speak to the old chief about the colours in the sky. Everybody else had laughed at her when she had said they were real things and could be handled, and had told her she was foolish to hope they might be brought down into the world to stay. But the old chief listened quietly to the girl's earnest talk, and when at last he smiled, it was not a smile of doubt or ridicule, but a kindly one that seemed to say, "all you have told me is very good." When she had done talking he answered, "My little snow-bird, let me tell you what happened long, long

ago, when I was young and strong, and my eyes were clear
and quick to see. There came into this village three birds,
much larger than our little friends whose name you bear.
One was the colour of the morning sun, another that of the
moon when she shines through the smoke of the burning
forest, and the other that of the clear summer sky. I saw
them as near to me as you are now. I could have shot
them with my bow, but did not dare. They staid a little
while and then flew away together. After they were gone,
as I walked under the branches they had perched upon, I
saw three feathers which they had let fall, one from each
bird. I picked them up and kept them. Though it is so
many years ago, I have them now. See for yourself that
these colours are real and true." Then the old chief opened
his medicine bag, took out a little roll of soft birch bark,
and handed it to the child. She opened it up with eager
fingers, and there lay, fresh as if they had fallen but yesterday, the feathers of the golden oriole, the scarlet tanager,
the bluebird, that had come to the chief in his youthful days
to teach him a lesson of faith.

Owistok gazed at the feathers with eager, loving eyes.
There were tears in them, but they were tears of joy. Now
she knew that the loveliness of the skies was no delusion to
mock the trusting heart, but something as real and true as
the sober browns and greens of the forests in which she
dwelt "Oh father," cried the girl at last; "why cannot
everybody, the old men and the warriors, the squaws and
the children, have such feathers as these to handle and look
at and adorn themselves with, till the world becomes more
beautiful? Will they not grow like the corn we put into
the ground in spring, and give us enough for all?" The old
chief answered, "No, my little snow-bird; "they cannot

grow. If we were to put them in the ground their colour would be washed out by the rain, and they would be bleached white by the sun. Very soon, my little pale-face, too soon for all our hearts, you will have more beautiful things than these. Then do not forget the people you have loved, but send us such colours as will grow." Owistok promised eagerly; then the old man rose, and, taking her quietly in his arms, laid her upon her couch of furs, where she fell asleep.

There was grief in the chief's house next morning. The old man took back his three feathers out of a little hand which would never open again, and put them away sadly in his medicine bag. The squaws moved quietly about their work, only sobbing as they looked upon a weary little face that yet wore a pleasant smile. There was neither fishing nor hunting that day. The children who knew no better cried for Owistok to come and play with them, and the older ones who knew could not comfort them. Everyone in the village felt that the world had suddenly became very empty. If a great chief had been taken away they could not have felt it more. But Owistok knew nothing of this. Very early that morning, it seemed to her, she had been awakened by the song of a bird, such a sweet song as she had never heard before. She rose up from her couch feeling strong and well, quite well, without any weariness or ache or pain at all; and she rose into a lovely summer day. What she wanted was to see the bird that had roused her with its song; and there it was, with crested head and shoulder tufts and plumes and long curling tail feathers of every rainbow colour, perched upon a tree beside her. She chirruped to the winged beauty as she used to do to the little snowbirds, and, like the tamest among them it came to her shoulder,

and even to her hand.   Then it would fly on a little before
her, singing when it stopped, to invite her to follow.   So on
they went along the sandy beach and among the forest trees,
tho bird leading her such a race as she had never run, all in
the bright sunlight too, and yet she was as fresh and strong
as when they started.   Then she saw that the bird must be
leading her somewhere, and did not wonder at it, because
the pretty creature seemed so wise.   Gladly she followed
and answered back its song with a voice as sweet and a heart
as full of joy.

Owistok and her little leader came at last away from the
lakeshore and the forest into a field of brightest green.   Then
the bird soared up towards the sky, and as her oye followed
him she saw, reaching far overhead, the rainbow arch she
had sought before in vain.   It was firm and solid as if made
of great transparent stones of every colour, and she longed
to set her feet upon it that she might give another proof how
real and true things beautiful were.   The bird came down
again and led her in a short time to the foot of the arch
which was not resting upon the ground, but built upon a
solid foundation that went down, how deep nobody can tell.
She set her foot upon it, trembling a little at first, as she
thought of disappointments before.   But it was firm and
solid as the everlasting hills, and soon she was running and
skipping like a fawn up its gentle incline.   She saw the
world beneath her growing very small as she ascended, and
looking forward saw the great white clouds that had seemed
so small when viewed from the earth, spreading out on every
side.   In a little while she was among the clouds that looked
like a great expanse of snow with little points of golden sunlight shining everywhere upon its surface. But it was neither
cloud nor snow ; it was a great mass of flowers, white, many-

petaled flowers, with golden-yellow hearts and great green leaves floating beneath them. Long purple and steel-coloured dragon flies and beautiful little birds flitted here and there and hovered over the blossoms which lay before her feet like a sea. O what joy filled the little girl's heart! She had found the colour that would grow. It was only white, indeed, and they had the white snow and the white bark of the paper birch down in the Indian village, but they had no flower like this. She touched the blossoms ; they too were real. She smelt their fragrance, sweeter than that of the Indian grass or the marsh hay in summer harvest time. Tenderly her fingers grasped the strong flower stalk that she might bring the lovely blossom closer to her face, that she might press it to her heart. She did not break the stem, but it came away in her hand as if it were a living, thinking and loving thing that knew how she loved it and wanted to come to her embrace. So one and another and another came to her until her arms were full, and the bundle of blossoms was large enough for her bird friend to perch upon and there warble his sweetest songs. Thus, with fragrant white lilies beneath and around her and clasped to her bosom, she went on her way over the rainbow arch.

Owistok passed over the great field of lilies after a while and saw the blue sky before her. She began to be afraid that the arch ended here, but the bird went forward singing gaily to let his little companion know there was nothing to fear. Then she regained her courage and went on to the point where the white ended and the blue began. Here was another joyful surprise. People might call the blue by the name sky or any other name they liked, but it was a bed of flowers all the same. Far as the eye could reach the flowers grew, blue as the waters she had tried to take into her hand. They were of two kinds : one rising, out of a sheathing leaf shaped like an Indian arrowhead, into a long spike around which the blue blossoms thickly clustered; and the other with a leaf like the bulrush, out of which sprang a straight and narrower stem crowned with three large showy petals that curled outwards and downwards from the golden throat like tongues. What could the little girl do with these new riches, brighter than the blue bird's feather she had held in her hand last night? Her arms were full already of the beautiful lilies. Then the thought of the feather made her think of the old chief's request, and her promise to remember the people she had loved and send them colours that would grow. So she looked down through a rift between the lilies and the flowers of blue, and saw the village from which she had come and the bay on the shore of which it was built just beneath. Kissing the flowers tenderly and breathing their fragrance again, she dropped them one by one through the rift in the sky, bidding them each go and make her friends happy and the world beautiful. Then she gathered the blue as she had gathered the white, till her arms were full, and went forward on her way. That night, though it was all day to Owistok, the people of the Indian village said that they saw stars falling from the sky. Many of the braves were frightened, but the old chief was glad, and said to himself, " Our little snowbird has kept her promise."

" If I have found such beautiful flowers already," thought Owistok, " what a lovely land of flowers there must be before me !" So she went forward with great hope in her heart. The walking had been very easy and pleasant so far, but now it seemed easier than ever. She had reached the top of the arch and was going down towards the western sky.

Soon that western sky burst upon her in all its glory. Only at sunset had she ever seen anything half so beautiful. A great field of crimson, yes of crimson blossoms, lay before her, and her bird was singing as if his heart were nigh breaking for joy. Just such a great joy sprang up in her own breast. She did not believe now in things of beauty, she did not hope any longer ; she knew, and the knowledge made her so happy that if she had been the same little Indian girl Owistok she thought she was, there would have been no room in her little body for the treasures of that happiness. She came to the crimson field. O lovely blossoms ! now dark and rich, now bright and glowing, with your expanded wings and long tails like birds of Paradise ready to fly away from your nest of light green leaves, with what bliss you filled that young child's heart ! The white was pure and fragrant, the blue fresh and beautiful, but the crimson is warm and generous ; it is her own colour, the colour of the love she shewed on earth so well. It makes her think of the loved ones, of the dark-haired maidens whom the flower would become, of the little children whom its beauty would attract in their most wayward mood, and of the old people who could place it before them in their homes as an image of the love that once had been and was to be theirs again in the Spirit Land. So she drops the blue blossoms one by one over the edge of the rainbow arch, and again with her prayers they fall like shooting stars down into the bay near the home where grief is not yet silent.

Her arms full of the crimson-scarlet flowers, Owistok goes forward, no longer treading the flowers down, but carried along as if she were a bird with wings ; and as she goes, the flowers appear more beautiful, the sunlight brighter, the world perfectly full of happiness. Not her one bird that led

her from the humble Indian cabin, but along with him a
thousand of brighter plumage and sweeter song keep her
company ; and as she nears the end of the rainbow arch she
hears wonderful notes like human voices bidding her welcome to everlasting joy.   She has come to the end of the
arch—no, not to the end, for the road seems to have no end,
but to the point where it leaves the world out of view, and
now is her only chance if she would share with her friends
below the treasures which have made her so glad.   Still she
can see the village, a little speck in the far off distance, and
somehow she does not want to go back again.   Besides, the
morning is not half over yet.   It is hard to part with these
red flowers, but then she thinks of her promise and her
friends.   Down they go, therefore, another heavenly shower,
and she gazes over the arch to see them fall safely and very
near her old home.   Then she rises with nothing in her
hands, and glad she is that it is so.   For before her is a
golden gate wide open, and within the gate are flowers and
trees so beautiful, so fragrant, so full of blessed life, that no
tongue can tell, no pen can write a word about them that
would be half the truth.   But why she is glad to be empty-
handed is because some one she has seen in her dreams,
and who seems to spring out of the rainbow arch itself, folds
her in arms of such love that her own arms are not empty
enough to throw around his neck, while he carries the little
snow-bird into the heart of the happy land.   That night the
old chief looks forth himself and sees the shower of meteors
falling from the sky.   " Owistok is thinking of us," he says
to himself ; " soon we shall see brighter things than my
three feathers."

A long year passes away.   The summer goes, and the
corn harvest follows ; the winter hunting season gives place

to the spring sugar-making, and then summer comes again.
Through that year there was one Owistok lying in the
ground under the forest trees, and another up over the rainbow arch in the happy land.   But Owistok under the trees
saw nothing, felt nothing, thought nothing either good or
bad, while Owistok in the happy land was full to overflowing
of the blessed life.   The day came round in the Indian village when the little girl went away just a year before.   The
old chief could not bear to stay at home that day, so he went
down to the beach and pushed his canoe out into the water,
and then paddled away through the long shallow bay into
the great lake.   There was not a cloud overhead, and the
waters were as blue as the sky above.   The sun was brightly
shining, but a light breeze helped to make its heat pleasant,
and rocked the little bark with the gently rippling waves it
stirred.   For a long time the old man paddled to and
fro thinking of Owistok, and wondering if the land to which
she had gone was more beautiful than the world he was in
just then.   "It is time my little snow-bird kept her promise," he said to himself, as he paddled home again.   Soon
he reached the bay and saw the village near its end.   But as
he skirted the bay not very far from the shore, he felt something that seemed to stop the way of the canoe, as a long
fishing-line held out from it or a floating branch would do.
He put his hand over the side as he turned the canoe half
round and caught hold of something soft and slippery.   He
pulled it in and found a great green leaf, quite round with a
narrow slit at one point running half way through till it met
the stalk.   This was something new.   Balancing himself carefully, the old chief peered with his dim eyes over the side of
his frail craft, and saw other leaves like the first.   But he
saw more; in the midst of them was a flower, a growing

colour, white with a golden heart ; and there was another, and yet another, floating on the surface of the water like ivory cups and spreading their fragrance far and wide. " Oh," he cried, " if my little Owistok were only here, what a happy child I should see ! what a bringer of joy this poor old useless man might become !" Aud then he bethought himself, and said : " But why should I grieve, for it is my little snowbird who has kept her promise and sent us down these pure flowers so like herself."

Soon the bow of the canoe was full of water lilies, and the wrinkled, grey-haired chief was smiling towards them like a child. He was near home now, and in a little while there would be joy and gladness in all the village he thought, and the people would remember the little girl who went away a year ago. He left the water lilies behind him, but still there was something that rubbed softly against the sides of his boat. Again his hand went over the gunwale, and this time up came a stalk with a broad green arrow for a leaf and a great spike of blue blossoms, so blue that the water looked pale beside them. " Owistok has kept her promise," the old man almost shouted, as he gathered in the flowers of the pickerel weed. Nearer still to the shore he found a few late blossoms of the blue iris that flowei s usually much earlier in the season. Then the canoe grated gently on the sandy beach full of floral treasures. He lands and walks a step forward, intending to call the boys and girls, that they may carry the treasures home, when his eye, dim as it is, falls on a little patch of green not far from the water's edge, which he has never seen there before. He stoops his aged form towards it. It is green below, indeed, but above it is the colour of blood, of the moon rising through the smoke, of the glorious evening sky. So, with a cry that echoes through the village and all along the shores of the bay, a cry of " Owistok, Owistok, you have kept your word," he gathers in the scarlet and crimson harvest of the cardinal flower.

Everybody runs down to the beach, the braves and the young men, the squaws, the girls, and even the children. They have heard the old chief's words and think that Owistok has come back again. Some, therefore, are much disappointed when they find the aged warrior radiant with joy among the blossoms. The braves look out upon the bay with its lining of lily pads and pickerel flowers, and declare that the fishing is ruined, and that game will never come near such a tangle of water weeds. A few careful squaws want to know if the flowers are good to eat, and when the old chief indignantly answers that that is not what they are for, they go away unconcerned. But the children ! how they revel in the colours, and ask for a yellow-hearted lily or pinky-white bud, for an iris, and, almost tremblingly as if it were too much to ask, for a single blossom of the cardinal flower. Then away they go with their prizes and bathe their young souls in the new-found vision of loveliness. The girls braid the long stalks in each others' hair, letting the flowers hang so skilfully that it is hard to tell which is the more becoming to these dark-eyed maidens, the pearly white or the deep sky-blue or the blood-red living ornament. Many a young man, too, does not disdain to break a thorn from a tree or take a porcupine quill from his dress, and with it pin to his hunting shirt of deerskin one of the tokens of Owistok's love. And the good old squaws, whose steps are feeble and their backs bowed with long years of hard work, pick up a flower here and there till one hand is full, then carry them home and set them in an unused broken cup, where the weary eye may be rested by the sight of them, and with their fragrance and beauty some joy may enter the heart.

" If our snow-bird can see us, how happy she must be,"
thought the old chief, as he entered the house with an armful
of treasures.   But he did not know that the Great Spirit was
looking down and rejoicing in the joy of his children.

That summer had been from the beginning very dry, so that
away from the water the grass was parched and the leaves
were commencing to shrivel on the trees.   There were forest
fires at many points on the lake.   You could smell the smoke
of them in the air and feel its smart in your eyes ; but the
breeze kept it away from the village.   Such a breeze was
blowing gently again, when next day the old chief with a
heart full of loving thoughts about his little snow-bird, paddled
forth into the lake.   But before he had gone far the wind died
away, and suddenly, like a great grey pall, the smoke came
down on every side.   So dense was it that he could hardly see
the bow of his canoe, and everything else was hidden from
sight.   Not even the sun, which often on smoky days he had
perceived like a little red ball in the heavens, could pierce his
way through the haze, or perhaps through the clouds above it.
The chief was all alone.   He thought of the way he had come
and tried to return upon his track.   Hour after hour passed
away, but he saw no sign of land, touched no rock, felt
nothing but the water which he dashed with his paddle and
the blinding smoke that made his aged eyes smart with pain.
Fiercely he struggled along, careless whether he wrecked his
little craft or no, the perspiration streaming from his forehead
with the violent efforts he was making.   Yet he came no
nearer home.   He knew that night had come though he could
see no stars, and all through that night he toiled until his
strength was well-nigh spent.   Then he lay down in his canoe
and washed his aching eyes and waited for day.

As the old chief waited, he thought of Owistok and of the

flowers she had sent down, which came like stars from heaven. Then he said to himself that the little snow-bird could never have found her way alone to the place where the flowers grew. The Great Spirit must have guided her safely and very quickly, since the falling meteors came so soon. So he looked up to where he knew the sky was, though he could not see it, and he prayed " Great Spirit, guide a poor old man, as you guided my lost Owistok home." Then he rose and took his paddle once more. And lo ! a star shot down, from what point in the heavens he could not tell, but it fell some distance in front of him. Towards the spot where the star seemed to fall he paddled his canoe. After he had gone a little space he felt something dragging or in some way hindering his course. He put his hand over the side and brought close up to his eyes the most welcome of all-sights, a water lily. He put his paddle down its full length in the water to feel for the bottom, but the paddle could not fathom the water's depth. Nevertheless he knew that the bottom was not far off and that land was near. Carefully now he felt his way, never leaving the bed of water lilies, though sometimes he went back and sometimes forward among them. Again in his heart he prayed " Lead me," and this time it was the blue flower of the pickerel weed which his hand grasped and brought into the canoe before his rejoicing eyes. " I shall soon be home now," he said, for the blue flower put hope into his heart. Now it was the pickerel weeds he would not leave. Sometimes they carried him back to the water lilies, and sometimes to the open water, but again and again he tried among them for the shore. At last his hand went forth and clutched another plant. He brought it up to his face and shouted for joy ; for its colour was that of the car- dinal flower, and he knew that it grew on the land. " Safe at home," he cried, and rose to his feet, then stumbled and fell, because he was very weary.

In an instant he was on his feet again. What a change in a single moment ! The smoke had cleared away, the sun was high in the heavens, and there, wonder of wonders, was little Owistok running to meet him, her arms all 'full of flowers, herself the loveliest flower of them all. He told her so, as he tenderly embraced his snowbird found once more ; but when she said that he was just as lovely and much nobler and grander, he would not believe, and said he was a poor old Indian whom the Great Spirit had made young. Then they went off hand in hand into the country of never-withering flowers and never-fading joys, to begin the blessed life that knows no ending.

In the Indian village, a squaw going down to the lake for water found the aged chief lying half out of the canoe, -with his face upon the ground in the midst of the cardinal flowers. The men came down and carried him up to his house and laid him on his couch, but he never spoke again. They wondered much how he had found his way home through the thick smoke that still lay like a dense cloud over land and water, and why there was such a happy look upon his quiet face. Then one of the women pointed to his hands. There, half-crushed by the paddle in the one hand lay a lily and a blue water weed, and in the other, fresh and whole, was the scarlet-crimson blossom of the cardinal flower. "These have guided him over the waters," she said, "and something like them must have led him to a happier home." Since that day, long, long ago, many an Indian has found his way by means of the flowers that Owistok threw down from the sky.

You would like to know what the flowers are, but I must first tell you what it is to be without the flowers and to want them. There is only One who is all true and beautiful and good, and that is God; and everything that is true and beautiful and good comes from Him. He has given us much that is beautiful in this world, but not enough to satisfy us or make us truly happy. Many people never think of anything better than the pleasures of this world, or, if they do for a short time, do not allow the thought to change their life. But others, like little Owistok, look away from earth to heaven. They see part of this heaven in their own hearts, which tell that God is pure and holy and good and that there is a blessed world beyond the grave for those who are like God. But the best and truest part of heaven they see in the Word of God, which shows us heaven itself and heaven shining on our earth in God's own Son and all the sons and daughters who have been made like Him. They long to have the glories of heaven, the beauty of holiness, in their own hearts and in the hearts and lives of all men, so that the world may share the beauty of heaven. So, in answer to their prayers and to beautify them and fill them with joy, God gives them the three flowers. The first is Faith, the pure white lily with the golden centre, for our faith has no colour at all but is just a hand that holds God's golden gift and believes all He says. The next is Hope, blue as the sky overhead, because it opens heaven before us. It is not one hope but many, like the pickerel weed and the iris; hope of being with God, of being like God, of having a place in His kingdom, of meeting our lost ones there, and many precious things beside. And last of all comes Love, blood red like the cardinal flower, for it comes from the heart and it gives the life to God, as God gave His Son's life-blood for us. When this flower comes into our hearts our heavenly bouquet is complete.

Faith tells us that God and heaven are near and are ours, though we do not see them; Hope tells us we are getting nearer, and paints before our eyes the joys of heaven; Love tells us that heaven is begun, for it is the spirit of Jesus Christ, the great Lord of heaven, in our hearts. Then let us live like the little Indian girl, so that through our lifetime the world may see these flowers adorning us and thus desire them, and that, when we at last cross the rainbow arch into heaven, the memory we leave behind may be like the blossoms which led the old chief to home and peace. And, above all, let us remember the flower that grows on solid ground. Few can know your faith, fewer still your hope, but love is visible to all. Therefore the Bible says : " The greatest of these is charity."

V.

Sir Aymer's Service for God.

V.

Sir Aymer's Service for God.

"Inasmuch as ye have done it unto one of the least of these my brethren, ye have done it unto me."—Matthew xxv. 40.

Squire Aymer was the only son of a French nobleman, who lived in the old days of chivalry. He was a goodly youth, tall, and straight as an arrow, handsome in feature, strong and brave; he was courteous in his manners, kind and generous to all, yet withal so full of lofty pride that he could not bear the thought of anyone having a higher aim in life than himself. As he had come to manhood's years it was time for him to drop the title of squire and take that of knight. Indeed he had already done many a knightly deed and well deserved the honour which, at any rate, was due to his father's son. But his loving father was an old man and feeble. He could not go with Aymer to the king's court and say to the monarch, "Here is my son whom I wish to be made a knight." One day, however, a visitor came to the castle and told them of a great court day soon to be held, when knights and squires from all parts of France were to appear and tilt against one another with spears before the king and queen and all the lords and ladies of the land. Rich prizes were to be given to the best tilters, and the young squires who did well in the ring were to be made knights by the king himself. When Aymer heard this he made up his mind to go to the court. His father gave his consent, and ordered his servants to make everything ready in the castle, so that his son might journey as it was fit for a nobleman to do and make a good appearance before the king. But the gentle Marguerite, who had been Aymer's playmate when he was a boy, and who was his father's ward because her own father had been his companion and had left her in his care when he died, this gentle Marguerite wept when she knew that Aymer was going away.

Squire Aymer was dressed in his father's best suit of armour which fitted him well, armed with sword and spear and shield, and his head crowned with a helmet of shining steel and golden ornament and nodding plumes. He mounted his favourite horse and, followed by a small company of men at arms, galloped proudly down the avenue, till his father and Marguerite could see him no more. A few days journey brought him to the court just as the sports were about to begin. When he came to the lists where all the knights and squires were waiting, a richly dressed herald asked his name and his errand. He answered that he was Squire Aymer, the son of a nobleman well known to the king, and that he had come to do brave deeds of arms, so that he might be made a knight by the king's hand. So at a sign from the herald, the warders opened a way for him into the ring where the tilting was to take place, and Aymer ranged his horse alongside of the other squires and made a finer figure than them all. Soon it was the turn of the squires to charge against brave knights who had seen service on many a battle field. Many a young cheek grew pale, and many a strong young arm trembled as they rushed across the field with such stout warriors before them. But Aymer's heart knew no fear ; his arm was as steady as if he had been at play. His

good horse bore him bravely on ; he caught his enemy's
lance upon his shield and turned it aside, while his own
stout spear, blunted though it was so that it might not
kill, made a terrible dent in his foeman's breastplate and
sent him reeling out of his saddle to the ground. Then,
as he leaped from his horse and helped the fallen knight
to rise, the people shouted, the ladies waved their kerchiefs
in the air, and the king asked the name of the brave young
squire.

Again on that day, and the next, and the next again, Aymer
fought, and every time he came out the conqueror. Then,
after the knights who had done bravely had received their
rewards, the heralds blew their trumpets and the chief of
them called upon the squires to come forward to the king.
There were only four that had won the honour of knight-
hood, and the first of these was Squire Aymer. Now it was
the fashion in those old days for a squire when he was first
made a knight to name some one whom he promised to love
and serve with a pure, true heart and willing hand, and for
whom he vowed that he would fight to the death against all
enemies. So the first squire that knelt before the king, who
was the last of the four in deeds of arms, chose the most
lovely lady in the court ; and when the king laid his sword
upon his shoulder and made him a knight, he swore that he
would always think of that lady, whether far or near, that he
would try to be worthy of her, and serve her if she needed
his service, and, above all, that he would do battle with all
who said there was anyone in the land more beautiful. The
next squire said he would love and serve the queen, for she
was the most noble lady in all the world. And the third
vowed to do battle to the death only for the king, because
he was greater even than the queen. At last it came Squire

Aymer's turn. He knelt before the king, just after an old priest, who had known his father, had spoken to him a few words in a whisper, and as he knelt. the old priest said aloud "my son, remember!" The king's sword fell upon his shoulder, and as it lay there Squire Aymer vowed that he would ever love and serve with true, pure heart and willing hand the great God of heaven who rules over all the nations of the world, and Him only, and that he would fight for Him to the death against all his enemies. Then the king said "Rise up, Sir Aymer, and keep your vow like a true knight;" but he wondered, and all who heard it wondered, at the strange promise Aymer had made. Many murmured, and said it was a pity that so goodly a young knight and so brave should turn his back upon the world as if he were a monk rather than a knight. Not so the old priest; he blessed Aymer and said, "God be with you my son, you have taken a noble vow."

The sports had come to an end. The king and queen were now in their palace, and many of the knights and noblemen were returning to their homes. Sir Aymer too was getting ready to leave the court, and thinking all the time of his vow. What should he do for God whom he had promised to serve? When would he see God whom he had sworn to love? These were the questions that rose in his mind and found no answer there. So he called his men together and rode towards home at the head of them, meaning when he reached the castle to ask his wise father these two questions, and, when he got the answers, to go anywhere and do anything that he might keep his plighted word. As he and his men were riding quietly in the heat of the day along a road through the forest, where the overhanging boughs of the trees gave them pleasant shade, they came to a place where a bridle-path in the wood joined the road, and out of this bridle-path came a little band of horsemen. Their leader was a strong looking knight, no longer young, whose sunburnt face, seamed with scars, showed that he had seen long service in war. But what made him differ from other knights Sir Aymer had met, was the sign of the cross which he bore upon his breast, on his shield, and even on the cloak that lay upon his horse's back. He bowed to Aymer and reined his steed up beside him, saying that he knew who he was, for he had seen him tilting before the king and had heard of the vow he made when he was knighted. Then he told the young knight that he was an officer in the service of Duke Godfrey of Boulogne, who was raising a large army to go to the Holy Land. "There," he went on to say, "is the place to serve God, for the Moslems who worship the False Prophet have taken the holy city, Jerusalem, and will not even allow poor Christian pilgrims to see the place where the Son of God was laid. Come with us and win back that holy sepulchre out of their wicked hands." Aymer did not know as much about Jesus Christ as little children do now, so he listened eagerly while the old soldier spoke of Him and of the Jews that crucified Him, and the Moslem Arabs and Turks who kept the land which His holy feet had trod. And when he heard that this Jesus was God's only and well-beloved Son whom He gave to the world to save sinners, Sir Aymer wished that he had lived in the Saviour's time, for then he would have seen God in His Son, and have learned how to serve Him. Then he thought, or else the knight told him, that he would be nearer God in the Holy Land than in France, and that it would be good service to fight against the enemies of His Son. So he told his new-made friend that he would join Duke Godfrey's army at

its place of muster, just before their roads parted. Then full
of this new thought he rode quickly towards his home.

Sir Aymer passed the days of his homeward journey in
a kind of dream, thinking ever of God and longing to see
His Son who had been, and if the old knight spoke truly,
still was a man like himself, only wiser, better, holier, God
as well as man. At length the castle upon the mountain
side facing the pleasant valley, came in view, and Aymer's
followers set up a shout when they saw it, so glad were
they to be home again. Sir Aymer remembered the time,
not very long ago, when he, too, would have shouted
with them like a school boy home for the holidays, but
now he had no home, no country, no king; God was in
all his thoughts and to him was everything. The welcome
he got was a grand sight to see. All his father's tenants
and vassals and servants were out to meet him, for Aymer
had sent one of his men home as soon as he was knighted
to give his father the news. And the loyal soldier had
told the old nobleman that his son was the handsomest
and bravest of all that fought in the lists, that the king
had given him high praise, and that he had taken the
greatest vow of all who had ever been made knights. So
the good old father's heart was glad, and right proudly
did he and Marguerite await the coming of the honoured
one whom they loved the best. But Sir Aymer took no
notice of the kindly people who cheered him as he rode
on, or of the little girls and boys that strewed woodland
flowers along his path, or even of the grey-headed steward
who stood at the foot of the castle steps to bid him welcome.
He took his father's proud, loving embrace very coldly, and
kissed the fair Marguerite lightly on the brow. Everybody
thought that he was vain and puffed up with his honours, so

unlike was he to his old kindly generous self. But he was not; he was very humble; he was thinking how he should serve God, and only God. There was no place in his heart for man or woman or child.

After his son had rested, the old nobleman questioned him about his vow, and was glad when he heard that it was so worthy a one and greater than all the vows made that day. But when Sir Aymer began to say that he must get ready to join Duke Godfrey's army and march against the Moslems, the good father's heart grew sore and he replied : " No, no, Aymer, you must stay with me. It will be only a little while, for I am old and feeble, and then you must take care of Marguerite." The tears came into Marguerite's eyes too, but she brushed them away when she thought nobody was looking and spoke bravely, though her voice trembled just a little, "Can you not serve God at home, Aymer," she said; " there are so many poor and weak people that need your kindness and your help? There are wolves and bears and other wild beasts to kill, and robber bands that will take away what the wild beasts leave, if you are not here to protect our villagers and husbandmen." Aymer only laughed a little bitter laugh, which he did not mean to be bitter, and said that young ladies could not be expected to know what was the duty of a knight, and above all, of a knight who had sworn to love and serve God, and Him only. Then Marguerite blushed and said nothing more, but went away to her little room to pray. Soon it was known all over the castle and in the village and among the country people, that Sir Aymer was going to the wars. The stout young men who were tired of cutting down trees and holding the plough were glad, and came to the castle to ask their young lord to take them for his soldiers. But the old people

and the weak ones and all the women and children came to
the old knight and Marguerite, and prayed them not to let
Sir Aymer go and take away their sons and brothers. All
their pleading was in vain. Sir Aymer said, " God wishes
it," and so he had his way. He led the young men into the
armory and clothed them with arms and weapons, while the
old people and the women went back to their homes
lamenting.

All too soon for many loving and sorrowing hearts came
the day of departure. Sir Aymer bade a cold farewell to
Marguerite, received his father's blessing, and rode away at
the head of a gallant company, proud to think that he was
able to lead so many soldiers to the holy war. As his horse's
hoofs were clattering down the village street, a woman ran to
meet him, crying through her tears, " Good Sir Aymer, my
child is lost; there are wild beasts in the mountains, and no
one left to search for him that can fight them. Stop, for the
love of God, and let the young men help me to find my
child." But Sir Aymer answered loftily, " My good woman,
I have greater work to do than to find lost children ; let the
old useless men attend to that." And so he rode away.
When he passed the long wood beyond the village he came to
a house in the fields, where another woman was standing at
the door. She, two, came out to meet him with tears in her
eyes, telling how her husband had been attacked by wild
boars when he had nothing to defend himself with, and, all
bruised and torn by their terrible tusks, had just managed to
crawl into the house where he now lay. She wanted Sir
Aymer to send one of his men to the castle for a doctor who
lived there, that he might come and heal the ugly wounds,
and besought him to do it for the love of God. " My soldiers
and I have a great work to do for God," he replied," and sick

men must take care of themselves." On again went the troop, the soldiers wondering what had happened to their young captain. They came to another forest outside of Sir Aymer's domain, in whose dark shades bands of robbers often lurked, and as they passed through they heard a feeble voice calling "Help, help, for the love of God." Some men-at-arms were starting for the spot, when Sir Aymer called them back. "We have no time," he said, "to heed every foolish cry. God's work is of more importance than an old man's money."

A few days' journey brought Sir Aymer and his band to the place of muster of which the weather-beaten knight had told him, and there he took up his station in the great host bound for the Holy Land. With many thousand knights and thousand upon thousand men-at-arms, he marched through many lands and crossed the little strip of sea that divides Europe from Asia in the south. In the old lands of Asia Minor and Syria he saw his comrades die in hundreds by Turkish sabres and javelins, by hunger and thirst and the fierce glare of a burning sky. Yet, still Duke Godfrey's army moved forward, beating all the Moslem forces that tried to bar the way, until at last it came to the walls of the Holy City. For five long weeks the army fought before Jerusalem, and then some brave soldiers climbed the high walls, drove back the enemy and opened the gates. Duke Godfrey and Sir Aymer and all the knights and captains rode in with spear and sword and battle-axe. The Moslems could fight no longer. They cried for mercy, but alas! the Christian knights, as they called themselves, thought nothing of the merciful and loving Christ whose name they bore, but killed all they met, as if the Arabs and Jews were wild beasts instead of men and women with priceless souls. Sir Aymer's heart was sick and sad with the dreadful sight, for he killed

no man in the city and would not let his own soldiers harm
the poor fugitives that crouched before them.   Right glad
he was when sunset came and the army ceased its work of
slaughter; when the savage warriors washed the blood from
their armour and went like a band of pilgrims to pray on
Calvary.

Sir Aymer found a large company praying in the Church of
the Holy Sepulchre, where it was said was the tomb in which
the body of Jesus once lay. Duke Godfrey was there kneeling
with the rest, and, when his prayer was ended and all the company was about to depart, each man to his quarters for the
night, he called Sir Aymer to him and gave the young knight
the honorable charge of guarding this sacred spot. Night fell,
and although there was noise enough in the city, all was quiet
in the church. Only one old priest was there, who went about
lighting some of the silver lamps that hung in the arches.
Outside, and just within the doors, could be heard the steady
tramp of Sir Aymer's sentinels, and he himself was lying upon
the paved floor, trying to sleep away his weariness. The old
priest was watching him, and when he saw that the knight
could not sleep, he came up to him and invited him to see the
place where the body of Jesus had lain. Sir Aymer rose right
gladly and followed his guide, who led the way with a lighted
taper.   Under the centre of the great dome they stopped, to
descend a stairway that led into a marble house.   From the
roof of this narrow building lamps were hanging.   The priest
lit one of these, and saying " This is the holy place," left Sir
Aymer there.   What thoughts passed through the young
man's mind of the great God whom he had vowed to love and
serve, and of God's Son who had walked in this very city of
Jerusalem, and had been crucified by wicked hands and laid
in this very tomb. " Oh ! if He would only come to me now,

that in seeing Him I might learn how to love God!" This was Sir Aymer's prayer. And I suppose as he bent forward, kissing the stone he thought so sacred, and forgetting all the world in his desire to see its Saviour, his old weariness must have come upon him and made him sleep. In his sleep he saw a vision of angels clothed in white. One of them touched him lightly saying, "Away, away, knight Aymer, this is not the place to find the Son of God; He is not here, He is risen; why seek the living among the dead?" Then the young knight arose and found that day had come, for drums were beating and trumpets calling the scattered soldiers to their posts. He returned to his old place in the church, and soon after, with many other worshippers, Duke Godfrey passed through the doors. Sir Aymer bowed low to the Duke, whom many already called King of Jerusalem, and said: "A boon, my lord; if I have deserved any favour from you." Godfrey answered, kindly: "There is no knight deserves more at my hands than Sir Aymer; what is the boon?" "That I may leave the army and seek elsewhere God and his Son whom I have sworn to love and serve," he replied, "for the murders of yesterday have made this city more like hell than the holy place where God dwells. I cannot find Him here." The Duke was sorry to lose the brave young knight, but he sighed as he thought how true was his saying, and wished him God-speed on his homeward journey.

Sir Aymer called his men at arms and told them he was going back to France. Very few were left now of the gallant company that three years before had sallied out of the castle gates so full of hope. The rest had fallen on the battle-fields and scorching plains of Asia Minor and Syria. Of those that remained only three were willing to go home with their young lord; the others liked better to stay in Jerusalem in

hopes of finding rich spoil to carry away in later years. So
their leader found service for them with a brave French
knight ; and then with his three companions set out on his
homeward way. There is no need to tell of his weary
journeys by land and sea. At last he reached Italy and
made his way into the region of the French Alps. One
evening he and his companions halted in a quiet valley
called Chartreuse, and looked about them for some place
where they might spend the night. They saw a building
not far off, the only one in the valley, large and new looking,
and towards this they turned their steps. One of the men
knocked at the door, which was opened by a monk, who
invited Sir Aymer to enter. As he went in, the monk told
the knight that the building was a Carthusian monastery,
which had been founded by the Abbot Bruno fifteen years
before, and that the rule of the monastery was very strict.
But what was Sir Aymer's surprise when his guide brought
him into the company of his brother monks, to find among
them his father's friend, the old priest who had spoken to
him at the court of the French king before he made his vow.
The monks were allowed to talk very seldom, for their time
was chiefly taken up with study and prayer and thinking
about God and holy things ; but this old brother, because
he was an old man, was granted more liberty than the rest.
So he gladly listened while Sir Aymer told his story of all
that had happened to him since the day they parted, how
he had always tried to keep his vow, but had not found God
or His Son in the Holy Land, and how a vision of angels
at the Church of the Sepulchre had warned him away and
told him not to seek the living among the dead. Then the
old monk told him of his own quiet life of seeking and
serving God, and drew such a lovely picture in words of the

quiet, pious life of the monastery with its prayers and reading of the Bible and other good books, and above all its
long thoughts of God and heaven, that Sir Aymer, tired of a
busy fighting life and of weary wanderings, cried out, "Oh
that I might have such a time of blessed rest!" "Come,"
answered the joyful monk, "and be one of us, for you have
already given up the world for God in your heart, and He
has promised to come to the humble and contrite and seeking soul. Come, my son, and here fulfil your vow."

That night Sir Aymer listened to the monks singing their
beautiful evening hymn and heard their solemn prayer, and
when he lay down to sleep he felt as if he were resting in a
very holy place. When morning came his soldiers were
waiting for him with his horse saddled and ready to mount.
But he bade them take his horse back again to the stable
and go their own way to France, leaving him in the monastery, for he was going to lead the holy life within its walls.
His faithful men-at-arms begged and entreated their master
to come with them, and spoke of their old lord, his father,
and the Lady Marguerite, who would be longing to see him
again. But he answered them "No, go your ways, and
may God bless you and them; for me, I have given up the
world and all its vanities." So the brave fellows went away
with tears on their rough cheeks, and the old monk blessed
the young knight again. The monks took off Sir Aymer's
armour and hung it up, together with his helmet and shield,
his sword and spear, in their hall as a trophy that they had
gained from the world. His horse they kept for the convent's use. And then they clothed him, who, a moment
before, had been a proud warrior, in a rough shirt of haircloth and a coarse black cloak, and led him to his cell with
its bed of straw. For a year, they told him, he would be

kept on trial, and then, if all was well, his name would be changed and he would be admitted as a brother. Now Aymer began to seek God and to try to serve him. All the hard tasks were given to him to do because he was the youngest in the convent. He had to chop wood, and mend clothes, to sweep out rooms, and even cook, as if he had been the meanest servant, but he never complained. When his work was done, he prayed and studied more earnestly than all the rest. So anxious was he to please God that he put the roughest haircloth shirt he could find next his skin and took the cloth covering off his straw pallet, that he might not rest too easily at night. So the months passed away in toil and weariness, for Aymer slept so little and fasted and prayed and suffered so much that he became pale and thin and weak. But what did that matter to him if only he might see God.

One day he found a book in the little library, written on parchment by monkish hands. When he began to read it he found that it was the story of God's Son, Jesus Christ. It told him all about the Saviour's birth, and miracles and preaching and sufferings and death. But there was nothing in it about monasteries and the kind of life he was leading. He read that Jesus told his scholars to go and tell poor sinners how He came to save them, and to do good as He did. What astonished him most of all was the place where it said that if anybody wished to serve Jesus he could do it by helping his poor friends, the hungry and thirsty, the naked and homeless, the sick and the prisoners; for what was done to them for the love of God was done to God Himself. And in another place it was written, " He that loveth not his brother whom he hath seen, how can he love God whom he hath not seen."

That night Sir Aymer confessed in prayer that he had not loved his brother, that is, his fellow man, as he should have done, and earnestly besought God to forgive him for the sake of Jesus Christ, and to show him how he must love and serve as he ought. And as he slept, there came to his spirit another vision of an angel form that said, "Arise and depart, for this is not your rest. The Lord Jesus did not pray that His disciples should be taken out of the world, but that they should be kept from the evil that is in it. Go and do the works of Him whom God sent." Then he arose long before it was day and went to the dining hall where his armour was hanging. He took it down and clothed himself once more like a knight. In the stable his horse neighed joyously to see him, and after he had put on its trappings and mounted, the faithful steed pranced about in the gladness of freedom. It did Sir Aymer's heart good to see the happiness of the dumb creature, and he thought of God who clothes the flowers of the field and feeds the merry birds that sing among the branches. But the Abbot was very angry because the young brother was going away, and the old monk wept bitter tears as he prayed him to stay. The knight thanked them for their kindness in taking him in, and answered their appeals by saying, "I must obey God rather than man, for Him only I serve. Read God's book and you will find that your's is not the best way to serve Him." So he left the dreary walls and rode away through the pleasant fields and forests towards France and his father's house.

Now he seemed to see God or something of God everywhere. The green trees overhead and the little flowers among his horse's feet, the scampering rabbits and the warbling birds, the rippling brook and the leaping trout in

its clear water, all seemed to have voices, voices that sang
in many pleasant holy tones, "God is good." The sky
became dark with clouds, the pattering raindrops fell, the
lightning flashed, the thunder roared, the little brook was
troubled and swelled into a torrent, the birds ceased their
song ; all was gloomy and terrible. But Sir Aymer got off
his horse and kneeled upon the ground in prayer, for he saw
God's power in the storm, and thanked God with uncovered
head that He had made him able to know something of
His greatness, and to love Him and trust Him in tempest as
well as in sunshine. Soon the wind swept the clouds away
from the face of the heavens and the sun shone forth again
bright and clear, making a rainbow athwart the sky. The
trees and flowers lifted up their dewy heads more fresh and
beautiful than before, and never had the song of birds
seemed so sweet to Sir Aymer's ears as then. His heart was
overflowing with love and joy. For every traveller he met
he had a kindly word and pleasant smile, so that many a
humble peasant man and woman and many a child looked
back again as they passed the gentle knight who had bade
"God be with them." That old father, how he longed to
see him and care for him in his old age ! And Marguerite,
his playmate of early days, would not be happier to welcome
him than he to be with her once more. "God be with
them," he prayed in the depth of his heart as he thought
how cruelly he had treated them both when he left his
home. Alas for poor Sir Aymer, they were both with God.
And so he soon learned, for when he came into France,
which was not so large a country then as it is to-day, he met
one of his old soldiers on the way to seek his master, who
told him the sad news. The good old nobleman and his
gentle ward had died long weeks before ; their bodies lay in

the tomb near the castle : their souls had gone in simple trust to God; and Sir Aymer was alone in the world,

So Sir Aymer knew what grief is, and such terrible grief as I hope may never darken your young hearts. He had lost those on earth whom he loved the best, lost them when he loved them most, and when he longed to be loving and helpful to them. They would never know how he looked forward to be with them, nor hear his humble confession of all the wrong he had done them in the past. His heart was very heavy and sore, but not so heavy that he could not lift it to God and pray for courage and strength and patience to do His will and bear his burden. God sent His heavenly comfort into the broken heart. Then Aymer knew that his father and his playmate were with God, and there he knew that he also some day would be, a thought which made him glad amid his sorrow. On he rode alone, for his old soldier whom he had met had gone elsewhere upon some errand, on to the deserted castle which was now all his own. He came to the dark wood outside of his domain, where years before he had heard the cry for help. This time he heard no voice, but as he passed through, his horse shied. Sir Aymer looked down, and there on the grass at his right lay the dead body of a man, a murdered man. He had been dead some days ; the murderous thieves had stripped him of half his clothes, and already the birds of prey had been there making their loathsome feast. Sir Aymer started when he saw the dead man's face, for it seemed to him that he had seen it before, yet where or when he could not recall. But he set to work to dig a grave for the body, because it was the body of a brother, although he had nothing but spear and sword with which to do the work. With his sword he cut the turf, and with spear he pried out the stones. Both sword and spear were broken before the task was ended, and then, wrapping the corpse in his cloak marked with the cross, he laid it tenderly in the new-made grave. At the head he set up his shield, and at the foot the fragments of his sword and spear to mark the place, and then he went forward on his way.

Riding on without sword or spear or shield, Sir Aymer came into his own lands. Here he was in the fields where the woman had called to him for help to her wounded husband. He saw the house out of which she came, and went up to it, meaning to ask the woman if her husband had recovered. But no answer came to his knock, and when he went in he saw a sick man lying upon a pallet of straw who faintly begged for water. The knight ran down to the stream and, washing his helmet, filled it with pure water and brought it to the fever-stricken patient who drank eagerly. He opened his eyes, and again it seemed to Sir Aymer that he had seen that face before. " Have you no doctor to attend to you," he asked ; and the sick man answered " No, but my neighbour would bring one to me if he had a horse, for the leech lives far away." Then the young knight went out and found a neighbour very like the man who was ill, and gave him his horse that he might go speedily and bring the doctor. But he continued his way on foot to the castle, intending to send help from thence to the sufferer. As he went on bareheaded, for he had left his helmet full of water by the bedside, he came near the village, and, on a stone by the wayside, saw a very little child, a mere baby, crying bitterly. The little child could only say that it was lost. Sir Aymer took the babe in his arms and soothed it with kind words. Nobody met him in the village. It seemed deserted. He climbed up

the hill to the castle, and that seemed deserted too. In he
went, however, for the doors were open, and, passing through
many halls and passages, came to what used to be his own
room. On his own bed he laid the baby, and sang it to
sleep with a gentle lullaby, putting his own gold chain round
its neck to play with, as it sank into a pleasant slumber.
Then, while the little child rested, he too, overcome by all
the labours of the day, too much for his feeble frame to bear,
laid his head beside the child, and with a prayer to God fell
asleep.

Daylight streamed in through the windows, and Sir Aymer
awoke, but the child was gone. The servants of the house
had come back, hearing of his arrival, and answered his call;
but none of them had seen the babe, and all thought that
the poor wasted knight was not in his right mind. He sent
them, for he was too weak to go himself, to carry food to
the sick man, and to ask if the kind neighbour had found
the doctor, and to bury the dead body in the wood as it
should be buried, and bring back his shield. A long time
they were away, but when they returned they said they could
find no sick man, no neighbour with the knight's horse, no
buried body in the dark wood. Then Sir Aymer marvelled
whether they were mad or he, and going to his room he
prayed God to make plain the mystery. Then, for he was
very weak and weary, he lay down upon his bed and went
to sleep. In this last sleep there came a vision of angels.
One bore a robe of dazzling brightness, saying "there is
your soldier's cloak;" another, a golden girdle, saying "this
is the chain that pleased the child;" another, a crown of
many precious stones, saying "this is the helmet that
moistened the sick man's lips;" and still another came who
stood by a chariot of glory, crying, "behold your steed that

shall carry you heavenwards." And then a kind, sweet
loving face, bearing the marks of human sorrow and sadness,
the same face he had seen in the dead, the sick, the lost,
but glorified ten thousand fold, bent above him ; a voice
soft and gentle and tender said "I have come to your
prayers Knight Aymer. Forasmuch as you have done it
unto one of the least of these my brethren, you have done it
unto me. Enter into the joy of your Lord.' So the Lord
kissed Sir Aymer, and with that kiss his soul went up to
God in Paradise. His servants came in the morning and
found him dead, with a holy smile upon his lips, and the
far off look in his eyes of the pilgrim that seeks his home.

When we learn the true value of the world and the glory
and goodness of God, we turn away from earthly things and
seek God with all our hearts. God is in all our thoughts,
but many of these thoughts may be very wrong, because
they are born of ignorance. Where is the Christian boy or
girl who has not longed to do some great thing for God !
Where is there one who has not wished to have lived in the
days of Jesus Christ and in his country, that he might have
laid down life for His blessed sake. How indignation against
His betrayers and murderers and against the foes of the
church in all ages has filled even youthful souls with what
they thought was zeal, but what was in large part a spirit of
revenge and hatred, quite unlike the spirit of the meek and
lowly Jesus ! In early Christian days the desire to do some
great thing for God sometimes led to useless martyrdoms,
and, in the later, to cruel persecutions and ungodly wars.
" Though I give my body to be burned and have not charity
it profiteth me nothing." But how shall we find God and

serve Him? Shall we leave the world and, being alone with God, come nearer to Him in heart and render Him a more acceptable service? No, for first we cannot get away from our sinful human nature in any place on earth, nor is it God's will that we should leave the world. "These are in the world," said Jesus, "and I come to Thee—I pray not that thou shouldest take them out of the world, but that thou shouldest keep them from the evil." In the days of His earthly life Jesus was found in towns and cities, and in them did most of His mighty works. So, now that He is exalted, though He is to be found by those who do their duty in quiet retreats, His more nearly felt presence is where the multitudes need His help. How shall we serve Him? He is the great healer. We can serve and follow Him by healing. He is the first comforter. We shall tread in His footsteps by comforting. He still goes forth to seek and to save the lost. In seeking them and in trying to save them, we shall come face to face with our Lord and Saviour. Then, at last, when we shall say, " Lord, when saw we thee an hungred and fed Thee? or thirsty and gave thee drink? When saw we thee a stranger and took thee in? or naked, and clothed thee? Or when saw we thee sick or in prison, and came unto thee? the king will answer and say, Verily I say unto you, inasmuch as ye have done it unto one of the least of these my brethren, ye have done it unto me."

VI.

The Fugitive of the South Seas.

The Fugitive of the South Seas.

"Thus saith the Lord, even the captives of the mighty shall be taken away and the prey of the terrible shall be delivered."— Isaiah xlix. 25.

Far away in the Southern Ocean lies the beautiful island Tahiti. As you approach it you imagine there are two islands instead of one, but coming nearer you perceive that the two are joined by a narrow neck. On one side of the neck the island is almost perfectly round and twenty miles wide every way, but on the other side it stretches out into an oblong, sixteen miles in length and eight in breadth. The centre of each of these peninsulas or half islands is full of mountains, covered, like the valleys and passes between them, with every kind of tropical tree and shrub. From the base of the mountains to the sea, a distance of two or three miles, the land is level, the soil rich and abounding in bread fruit and cocoanut trees, with plantations of yams and taro roots and other plants that are good for food. In the old days, long before white men came in their great ships to visit the islands of the South Seas, and even before some of the islands had been heaved up from the depths of the ocean by volcanic fires, there reigned a mighty monarch in Tahiti, named Taaroa. He had the best right to rule there, for it was he who had called the island up from its watery bed, and all the people who dwelt in it were his children. These people were brown of skin and black haired, but the men were tall and lithe and strong and handsome as many of their descendants are to-day, and the women were graceful in form and beautiful in feature. Sickness was not known among them. No thieves passed through the ever open doorways to steal. No wild beasts lurked among the mountains to devour. The earth brought forth almost without man's help all that was needed for daily food. The bamboo furnished wood for house-building, and its large joints, hollow above and below, could be made with little trouble into vessels for eating and drinking. The women wove long grass and fibres into mats of varied colours and tasteful patterns, and made delicate native cloth by beating thin the inner bark of the mulberry tree. Peace reigned throughout the happy island. In their songs the people tell even now how the king sat in justice and kindness on his great stone seat, while the spreading roots of the bread fruit trees were shaved off clean on the paths and polished with pumice stone from the mountains; how all the men were strong, the women beautiful and the children good, with nought to trouble their rest or make them afraid.

King Taaroa reigned over Tahiti, but that island was only one and a small one among his many possessions. North and south, east and west, his empire extended. There is hardly an island even now in the southern seas in which his name is not known, either as Taaroa or Taaloa, Tangaroa or Tangaloa. His servants brought him tribute from the rugged mountain islets and the low coral strands, from the homes of the tufted haired blacks and those of the sleek, oily yellow and red men. At Manuka, in the far west, his beloved son Karika stationed his fleet of great canoes, which swept over every sea, exploring new lands and bringing all into subjection to the Tahitian king. But there was another fleet besides that of Karika, which often appeared off the shores of Tahiti, though it never landed on any beach. The islanders saw it, but did not fear, because they knew of nothing wrong, and saw no reason why this strange fleet should do them harm. Still they were anxious to know who the men were that manned its many canoes, and why they had never set foot on their king's domain. Now the chief man on the island after the king was Tangiia, a brave, handsome and wise prince, into whose care Taaroa had given almost everything and everybody in Tahiti. There was one thing that Taaroa would not give him. It was a huge bread fruit tree which towered to a great height above the others round about it, and then, spreading widely on every side, displayed far out of reach its strange flowers in sheaths or naked catkins and its large round fruits, which on this particular tree were of every brilliant colour. Now, just because he could not get it, this great tree was what Tangiia most desired. It grew on a point near the sea shore, a point often passed by the strange fleet which had excited the people's curiosity. Many a time did Tangiia go down to that point and look up at the glowing fruit so far out of his reach.

One day Tangiia was standing by the beach looking up at the tabooed tree, for so it was called, since all that the king kept for himself was known as taboo or forbidden. As he was looking longingly towards the great coloured globes shining in the sunlight, the strange fleet appeared, and for a moment remained motionless in the calm, blue water just before him. A large, dark looking, ill-featured man sat in the stern of the principal canoe, and although Tangiia did

not like his looks, he called out, " Who are you, and why do
you not land on this island !" The dark man laughed a
harsh, grating laugh, and answered, " Eat the fruit of that
beautiful tree and you will find out who I am, and, more
than that, when you have eaten I will land on the island
and be king instead of Taaroa. So saying, the dark, name-
less man went on his way and Tangiia was left alone. Now
a fierce desire possessed him to taste the luscious looking
fruit, so that his mind had room for no other thought. He
could not reach the fruit nor could he climb the tree, for
many thick and wide spreading branches stood in the way.
So he hastened home and got his axe. He saw Taaroa on
the road as he returned, but stepped away out of sight
among the bushes for fear he should be stopped and questioned. He had never been afraid before, but now he trembled in every limb as he looked about to see that nobody
was watching him. Then he came to the tree and began to
chop. To his delight the trunk was soft and green, so
that his axe made no noise and sank deep into the wood at
every blow. Yet so thick was it that more than an hour
passed before he reached the centre. A few cuts on the opposite side towards the water made the tall stem shiver, and,
after a few more, it began to bend towards the sea. As it
gradually inclined its lofty head Tangiia caught the fruit
within his grasp and put it eagerly to his lips, tearing away
the outer shell with his teeth. Alas for the deluded man, it
was full of ashes and bitterness. He tossed it away in
disgust and repented of the wickedness he had done, but it
was too late. In another moment the giant stalk broke
asunder and, with a crash that shook the island like an
earthquake, it fell to the ground.

Tangiia stood rooted to the spot. Soon a mocking laugh

aroused him and there, no longer in his canoe, but standing on the solid ground, was the dark man who had advised him to eat the fruit of the now fallen tree. "You wished to know who I am, he said; I am the great Tutabu, once the servant but now the enemy of Taaroa. I have landed because you have driven Taaroa away by your brave action, and now I can be king of Tahiti and your lord and master. Carry me to the great stone seat and tell all the people that I am their new king." Hardly knowing what he did, Tangiia took the rebel Tutabu on his shoulders and carried him towards the great stone seat, followed by the rebel's servants, who had left their canoes on the beach and came after their master with horrid yells and shouts of war. When the stone seat was reached, Tangiia saw that Taaroa had indeed gone, and far over the sea he noticed a large white canoe skimming the surface of the water. In that canoe he knew that Taaroa was journeying to the west. But the people had gone also. They had heard the fall of the great bread fruit tree and had seen the departure of Taaroa, and their blood had curdled at the sound of the shouts and yells made by Tutabu's followers. So in a body they had left their homes and fled for safety to the mountains. When Tangiia saw the desolate empty homes of his people he uttered a terrible cry and tried to shake his new master from his shoulders, but Tutabu clung to him all the tighter and drove his knees into the poor man's sides and kicked him so, that Tangiia, who had never before felt pain, was very sore. "Remember," said the wicked Tutabu, "that it is useless to try to get away from me. The only one who could deliver you is now your enemy, because you have disobeyed his orders. My orders I will take good care that you shall never disobey." So he called some of his servants to him and gave Tangiia into their care with in-structions to bind him with thongs while he sat like a king upon Taaroa's throne. So the guards laid hold of the cap-tive prince and led him away to the base of the mountains, because a tree grew there whose bark was tough and supple as a leathern thong. From this tree they stripped the bark and prepared to bind their prisoner hand and foot.

While Tutabu was sitting on Taaroa's throne and giving himself out for King of Tahiti, and while his servants were preparing to bind Tangiia, who had brought mischief to the island by his folly and wickedness, the true king was sailing over the ocean to the west. Soon he arrived at Manuki, and there he was met by his son Karika and the great fleet he commanded. "My son," said Taaroa, "I have left Tahiti because Tangiia has brought rebellion into the island, and will soon make all the people rebels in heart. Tutabu has heard of my absence and has taken possession of the kingdom and people. But I still love Tangiia, though he is a rebel, and wish to save him. Will you help me?" Then Karika answered "My father, your wish is my wish, and your heart my heart; my ships are your ships, and my war-riors your warriors. Send me where you will." So Taaroa told Karika to go into the south and find a new home for Tangiia and his people; then to return in the direction of Tahiti and meet the rebels and bring them to their new home. "And I," said Taaroa, "will go to Bolotoo and from thence will send help to Tangiia, that he may escape from Tutabu." So Karika called his canoemen and warriors together and embarked with them in the fleet and sailed away into the south towards the distant island of Raratonga. And Taaroa went away like a flash of light in his canoe, that glided over the waters without sail or paddle, to the wondrous island of Bolotoo in the north-west, an island that no living man has ever seen without bidding farewell to all the world beside. There he prepared help against the call of his disobedient servant Tangiia, whom he yet loved with a very great love.

Now let us go back to Tahiti. There is Tutabu on the great stone seat, giving himself out for king of all the world, and there is Tangiia in the hands of this monster's servants, waiting to be bound. He hears a flutter of wings and looks upward. Just above him hovers a wood-pigeon, a beautiful creature, whose feathery coat is all ablaze with vivid ever-changing metallic hues. It has something in its beak like a little fruit. Tangiia gazes in astonishment and with mouth wide open at this strange witness of the cruel scene in which he is a victim; and as he gazes open-mouthed, the tiny fruit falls between his lips sweet as honey, cool and refreshing as the cold spring waters. Then the bird flies back towards Bolotoo. The servants of Tutabu have seen nothing of this. They have been so busy with the thongs and are so satisfied that their prisoner is too weak to resist them, that they have not taken the trouble to watch his every movement. And he was weak a moment ago, that great strong man that used o be ; but he is not weak now, for that little fruit has put great strength into his heart, and the heart has made the body strong as well. They begin to bind him, but he snaps the thongs asunder, scatters his persecutors right and left, and, while they are calling for Tutabu to come to their help, he darts away and flees to the mountains whither his family and all his people are gone.

Next day a great chase began. Tutabu was exceedingly angry to find that Tangiia had got away for the present, but he was sure of capturing him and all his people in the end, for there was no way of escape from the island. Collecting all his followers he set out over the mountains. Tangiia meanwhile had found his friends and had made preparations in case of pursuit. His sentinels, posted upon high ridges of rock that seemed to touch the clouds, spied the host of Tutabu approaching and gave the alarm. Then the fugitives went on to higher ranges and over ravines and water-courses and into caverns that opened out upon the shore, but always with Tutabu close behind them. They could hear his voice at times calling out " Who cut down the great bread-fruit tree ? Who disobeyed Taaroa ? Let him not think to escape from me, for Taaroa will not help him." So they went on through the length and breadth of the island, Tangiia and his party fleeing in terror, and Tutabu with his followers pressing close upon their footsteps. At length the fugitives became very weary, for there were many old people and women and children among them, while Tutabu's party was composed entirely of fighting men. Tangiia stood in despair by the shore at the western end of Tahiti, surrounded by a company of terror stricken men and weeping women and helpless children. They could do nothing more, and close behind them, so that their wild shouts and even the cruel words they spoke could be heard, came the dreaded Tutabu. Then Tangiia cried in despair "O Taaroa, if you were only here, this evil being would have no power to harm your children. Will you not save us ?" And lo ! at that very moment a great canoe, carried in the air by myriads of brilliant feathered pigeons, descended from the west towards the shore, with out-riggers and paddles and masts and strong mat-sails all complete. The birds left it there half in the water, and, rising like a cloud of green and crimson and gold into the air, they uttered their cooing note of peace and gentle-ness, and flew away to Bolotoo from whence they had come.

Quick as thought Tangiia ran to the canoe and his people with him. The children and women and old men were got in. Then the young men stood on either side, the outermost above their waists in the water, and, at a call from Tangiia, they slid the huge boat into the sea, clambered over the gunwales, and worked the smooth well-made paddles with a will. Tutabu rushed down to the beach and shook his fist towards them in helpless rage, while his followers howled in doleful company. But Tutabu had canoes, though they were some distance away, and, as Tangiia's party looked back, they saw the dark-faced rebel leading his men towards the fleet. So they paddled with all their might, and when the breezes blew morning and evening hoisted their slender masts and mat-sails and ran before the wind. The canoe seemed almost to steer itself in a north-westerly direction towards Bolotoo. It made rapid progress, and very soon its occupants came to Huahine, an island a hundred miles from Tahiti, and something like it in appearance, though very much smaller. The fleet of Tutabu was nowhere in sight, so Tangiia and his people landed and began at once to prepare their dwellings and gather food. That evening they ate and drank in peace, and through the night enjoyed a pleasant sleep, but when morning came the watchmen on the hills gave the alarm, and, hastily gathering a supply of fruit, the party re-embarked, for the avenger was on their track and not far behind them.

Away again over the sea went the great canoe. All were refreshed with food and rest, so that the paddlers worked vigorously and soon put a long distance between their vessel and the pursuing fleet. This time the canoe went straight to the west, and, in a much shorter space than it had taken to come from Tahiti to Huahine, it reached another some-

what larger island of the same mountainous character and
beautiful aspect, called Raiatea.   Again, because the enemy
was nowhere to be seen, Tangiia landed, and with his people prepared to make a new home.   But their respite was
very brief, for before the mats were laid for the night's rest
the fleet of Tutabu appeared in the east, and all was hurry
and confusion to get back into the ship.   All that night they
paddled and sailed northwards in hopes of putting their
enemies off the track.   They passed Tahaa by, because it
offered no shelter and next day saw Porapora.   The sea
had become very rough, and they were afraid lest their vessel, large as it was, should be swamped by the surging
waves or dashed to pieces against the rocks.   But as they
came nearer, they found that Porapora was a little rocky
island in the centre of a wide basin of calm water.   A circular coral reef surrounded this basin, and against this reef the
huge waves expended their force in vain.   Then they watched
the fish and saw that, while some of the flying fish darted on
the crests of the waves over the low lying parts of the reef,
great shoals crowded into a narrow opening.   Towards that
opening they turned the bow of the canoe in faith that there
was a channel there, and happily their faith was just, for
after two or three great breakers had lifted the vessel high
in the stern and made the fugitives fear that their end had
come, the boat slid into the calm, quiet water, in whose
transparent depths they could behold with pleasure and restful hearts all the wonders of the sea.

Here then Tangiia and his companions determined to
stay.   So while some of the young men built their bamboo
huts and helped the women to gather roots and fruits for
food, he and the rest collected great stones and carried them
in the canoe to the opening in the reef.   Load after load

they carried until they had filled up the breach, and rejoiced to see the wild waves dashing over their wall just as they did over the solid reef itself. Now the poor hunted Ta- hitians had no fear. They ate and drank and were merry. They slept that night without sentinels, and when the morning came and they looked out upon the sea, they were rather glad than otherwise to behold the fleet of Tutabu approach- ing. On came the fleet. Tutabu was there at the prow of the foremost canoe, already exulting in the thought that he had got his enemies into a net from which there was no escape. As he saw the people standing quietly upon the shore, he imagined that they were too much exhausted to make any further efforts, and that they intended to submit to his authority. But when he came near the reef he was foiled. He could not remove the barrier wall, for the great waves would have dashed his canoes to pieces in the attempt. Yet he would not give up his prey. Part of his fleet he sent back to Tahaa for provisions, and with the rest he sailed round and round the reef, looking in vain for some opening into the lagoon. Tangiia and his friends rejoiced. They shouted across the lagoon and the reef at their highest pitch of voice, taunting their enemies and asking why they did not come on and make them their slaves. Tu- tabu ground his teeth with rage and waited.

Next day a great storm came on from the south, toss- ing the pursuing canoes so violently with the force of winds and waves that Tangiia expected to see them sink or break into shivers on the reef. But Tutabu was a cunning sailor. He made for the northern side of the reef and lay there quietly. Soon the storm went down, as suddenly as it had arisen. Then returning to his former position, he saw to his great joy that the storm had done what he could not accomplish.   It had swept Tangiia's rocks out of the breach as if they had been sea shells or pumice stone.   Stealthily his canoes passed through the opening, one by one, his own leading the way.   The followers of Tangiia were asleep, for it was early morning when Tutabu entered the lagoon.   In a moment they awoke with terror, for the awful shouts and yells of their enemies were in their very ears.   Hastily they started to their feet and made for the shore, but not before many of them had fallen by blows of murderous club and spear, and others had been bound and made prisoners. Tangiia escaped, and with the rest of his people fled to the ship.   With desperate strength, though diminished in numbers, they pushed it off from the beach, where it had lain high and dry in the hope that it would never be needed again.   They heard the dreadful cries of their wounded and imprisoned companions, but dared not stay to help them lest they should meet with the same fate.   Away through the broken reef they sped, paddling with all their might, and after them in hot pursuit went Tutabu and his fiendish warriors.

On to the west the great canoe skimmed over the waters. The terrible cries and wailings of their companions still rang in the ears of the paddlers, and made them work with all their might.   After a long and weary voyage, which taxed their strength to the utmost, another island like that they had left, but much smaller, came in sight.   It was Maupiti, and it, too, had a barrier reef and a quiet lagoon within. Into this lagoon Tangiia steered the ship, and once more he and his comrades sought rest on solid land.   This time they did not attempt to bar the way.   Instead, they kept watch by turns, and when they rested it was like soldiers ready to move as soon as the drum should beat or the bugle blow.

But they did not simply watch. They also worked, for a bright thought came into Tangiia's mind, and that thought was a scheme to put Tutabu off his course. He had looked to the north from a high point of land, and had seen an island there; to the west, and in that direction had seen two or three; while in the east, from which he had come, they were very numerous. But away in the south there was no land visible. So Tangiia determined to fill the empty space of the great ship with provisions for a long voyage, and to trust himself and his companions on the open sea. So, great stores of breadfruit and cocoanuts, with many other roots and fruits such as the taro and the banana, were collected and stowed carefully away under planks and mats that would shield them from the heat of the sun. Water casks were made out of the hollow joints of bamboos and sections of the trunks of larger trees out of which the pith could be easily removed, and these were filled with fresh water from the clear cold island springs. Turtles also were caught and laid on their backs where they could not move, waiting for the appetites of their captors; and grass nets, lines made of fibrous roots, bone fish hooks, and long, barbed fish spears were prepared to furnish the little company with food on the way from among the flying fish and other wandering tribes of the sea. Flat stones, suitable for a hearth and oven, were put on board the ship, so that the fugitives might cook their meals, even while they were out upon the ocean fleeing before their enemies.

Still Tangiia waited. He hoped that Tutabu would give up the chase and go back to rule over Tahiti with his wild servants. But Tutabu had no thought of giving up the pursuit. He was a hunter of men and cared nothing for

8

the beauties of Tahiti without the people who had once
been happy there. Just as soon as Tangiia had finished
his preparations, one of the men on the lookout cried,
"Here comes the fleet." And so it was. Tutabu and his
followers appeared in sight, and their canoes were being
paddled in great haste with the intention of cutting off the
retreat of the fugitives. Tangiia at once called his people
together. They entered the large ship and paddled out of
the lagoon before Tutabu's eyes. Then, to his great amaze-
ment and annoyance, instead of going to the north or west,
the Tahitians directed their course southward into the
trackless sea. Tutabu had no provisions and dared not
follow them. He had to land upon Maupiti to refresh
his hungry, thirsty and tired warriors, and while he was
doing this the great canoe sailed far into the south. The
rebel chief knew, however, that by sailing to the west he
would fall in with a chain of islands that would bring
him also to the south by easy stages, and in this way he
determined that he would, in the long run, come up with
those who had baulked him again and again. So after
he had staid a short time on Maupiti he went to sea
and made his course westward and southward by Mo-
pelia and Aitutaki.

There was great joy in Tangiia's company. The weather
was fine, the seas calm, the breezes gentle and soothing.
They had all the food they needed, and their vessel was
large enough to allow of their sitting, lying, standing or
even walking about at ease. Day after day they looked
out to the north, but their eyes saw nothing of their
dreaded enemy. Neither did they see any land, but often
they saw land birds flying overhead and stray turtles on
their way to distant islands, and once they were terrified

with the sight of an enormous lizard basking on the top of the waves in the sun. It was a wandering crocodile, all the way from the Indian seas. These told them that land could not be very far away. One morning Tangiia rose from his couch of mats refreshed with pleasant sleep and rejoicing in the feeling of safety that had been growing day by day upon him and his people. As he was taking his morning repast of fruit he heard a sound of wings overhead, and looking up saw a large flock of pigeons, the very same, it seemed to him, that had brought the great canoe upon their brilliant backs from Bolotoo. They greeted his gaze with their cooing notes so full of peace and affection that Tangiia thought they had come to say how glad they were that he had escaped from his enemy. Away went the shining flock into the south, and his eyes somehow were compelled to follow. But what is it he sees there besides the doves that makes him start and that sends paleness even into his tawny cheeks? It is a fleet of great canoes, each one larger than his own. Can Tutabu have found his way down there so quickly, and if it is he, from whence has he got these large vessels? No, it cannot be Tutabu. What will he do? He turns to his people all awake and gazing with terror in their eyes in the same direction. He asks them "What shall we do?" To go back is to fall into the hands of Tutabu and his cruel servants. To go forward is to become the prey of this new enemy.

The boatmen cannot paddle either way in their fear. The canoe lies like a log in the calm sea. There is weeping and wringing of hands among the women and the feeble ones. But nobody dares to give advice. They stay where they are waiting for their fate. Quickly the great fleet skims over the water. The fugitives can see the crews of the canoes, and watch the strong quick strokes of the paddlers, and in the stern of the foremost vessel, seated upon a throne on the lofty poop, they behold one who must be a very great chief, so grand and majestic is his air, and so rich his feathered cloak of every glancing hue. "It is Karika!" says one and another of the fugitives, as they remember what Tangiia has done in the realm of his father, Taaroa. Then they hide their heads in their mantles and wait for death. Now Karika's canoe comes alongside. In a moment the paddlers hold the water, and in another the two canoes are lashed together with thongs. Then Tangiia finds heart and voice in his despair. "My lord Karika," he cries, "we are your captives; all that we are and all that we have is yours, for we flee from your enemy and our enemy, the demon Tutabu. Better that we should fall into your hands than into his." All the people find their voices too and join their prayers and promises with much weeping and lamentation to those of Tangiia. Then Karika waves his hand to the warriors, who stand with one foot in their own canoe and the other on the gunwale of Tangiia's, ready to strike with sword and spear. At once they lower their weapons, and wait their chief's command. "Do you speak truly, Tangiia," he asks : "would you not escape from me if you could, and do harm to my father's dominions again?" Then Tangiia answers, "My lord Karika, it is impossible to escape from you, for is not the very ship in which we have fled from our great enemy a gift from the land of Bolotoo, that no man has seen, and over which your father rules, against whom I have sinned? Receive me and my people as your servants for ever." So saying he bowed his head before Karika till it reached the gunwale beneath that great chief's feet; but

Karika bent down, took the penitent man by the hand, and lifted him up. "Be faithful," he said, "and all will be well."

At a signal from Karika, thirty-nine strong rowers left his warship and took their places in Tangiia's canoe, and twenty-seven gentle, kindly servants, laden with provisions and comforts for old and young, followed them. The warm, ill-tasting water in the casks from Maupiti, with the decaying fruit and hardened cocoanuts they threw overboard, and fed the now joyful fugitives with fresh food pleasant to the taste, and gave them water to drink, cool and limpid as that from mountain springs. All that day the people rested and feasted while the thirty-nine rowers and twenty-seven servants attended to all the wants of the ship, and made it rise and fall gaily over the gently heaving waves. Karika was ever alongside of them in his great canoe, and all round about them were the vessels of his mighty fleet. On to the west they journeyed together, and came after some days to the island which Karika had prepared for the rebellious servant of his father, the beautiful island of Raratonga. Tangiia saw with delight the spacious and safe harbours, the green shady shores, the ranges of mountains towering one above the other towards the sky, and the lovely valleys among them, every one of which was like a glimpse of a fairy world. Here the fleet halted and the crews landed. The followers of Karika worked with Tangiia's people not in putting up mere tents for a few days stay, but solid and substantial houses to last for many long years. But Tangiia and his people had the special honour of building a house for Karika. In doing this they spared no pains, for had they not surrendered themselves with all their strength and possessions to that gracious chief. Then the land was portioned out and the work of cultivation began. Tangiia dwelt on one side of the island and Karika on the other. Part of the time Karika's people worked for Tangiia, and part of the time Tangiia and his people worked for Karika. So very soon the island became a perfect paradise of beauty and fruitfulness, and the two peoples lived together in the utmost peace and harmony. All Karika's thoughts were to do good to Tangiia, and Tangiia's efforts were in all things to please Karika.

In the meantime, what had become of Tutabu. He took a long time to make the circuit trom islan·l to island, and met with many mishaps by the way, but never shrank from his purpose of overtaking the Tahitian fugitives and making them his slaves. He heard that Karika's fleet was on the seas, but he never dreamt that Karika would befriend the man who had been the means of sending Taaroa away from Tahiti. Indeed he fully expected that the sight of Karika's vessels would be enough to make Tangiia return and fall into his hands an easy prey. So he pressed forward. After a long sea-voyage, his fleet reached Aitutaki, and thence he sailed or paddled southwards to Manuae. Another stage brought him to Takutea and another to Atiu. Here he rested awhile, for the stretch of open water to the south was broad. Having provisioned his ships and provided his warriors with new arms, he at last made his way towards Raratonga, where he had a suspicion that he would find those he was in pursuit of. At last he sighted the high mountains of ·the beautiful island. Tutabu was determined not to let his prey slip out of his fingers this time. His fleet remained out of sight of Tangiia and the other dwellers on the island till nightfall, and then, when all the rest of the world was asleep, he and his cruel followers glided stealthily in their canoes over the calm waters towards the new settlement. When the pursuing fleet arrived in the harbour, the warriors rested on their paddles and waited for the early dawn to begin the attack. But there was a man in Tangiia's village whom Tutabu did not expect to find there. He was one of Karika's men, and his name was Mataara. Like the Norse Heimdall he slept more lightly than a bird, and had so fine an ear that he could hear the grass growing in the valleys and the fish swimming in the sea. Like him also he carried a great trumpet in the shape of a long spiral shell, the sound of which could be heard for many miles. Mataara was listening while Tutabu's fleet came over the water. As soon as it came into the harbour and the paddlers rested for daylight, he ran to Tangiia's tent and cried softly " Awake, awake, Tangiia, for your enemy has found you out." Then Tangiia arose and gathered all his fighting men without noise. Among them were those whom Karika had sent to help him, the thirty-nine stout rowers and the twenty-seven kind attendants. But lo ! the twenty-seven who had appeared so mild and gentle before were now the most warlike in Tangiia's battle array. Quietly they marched down to the beach and waited too for daylight.

Soon the sky in the east became pale, and, as the night mists rolled away, the light was warm and rosy of hue. A little more waiting and the sun arose in his golden splendour, revealing the two war parties to each other. Tutabu and his men gave a fiendish shout as Tangiia and his people pushed off their one canoe from shore, but their shout was returned by such a blast from Mataara's trumpet as made Tutabu tremble. The sound of the trumpet rang clear over all the island, and echoed from the rocky mountain tops far out upon the sea. Tutabu trembled, for he had heard that trumpet before and had suffered from its blast, but he would not give up the fight. He hoped to be able to capture the trumpeter and teach him a lesson, as he had done to other trumpeters who had made as much noise, although their trumpets had not the clear true ring of this one. On he came with his fleet. and out to meet him came the ship of Bolotoo, with Tangiia poising his long spear in the bow, and his warriors ready for the fray. Then when they met there was a dreadful battle. Tangiia and his men fought bravely, but many a time he would have lost his life or been taken prisoner if one or more of the thirty-nine or the twenty-seven had not dashed in between him and his opponents and driven them howling back into their canoes with painful wounds. The enemy was too strong for Tangiia. So many were Tutabu's canoes that, when one was driven off, another came forward full of fresh warriors eager for the fight. At last they surrounded his vessel and hemmed him in on every side. Then Mataara sounded his trumpet again, and almost before its notes died away a shout was heard like that of a mighty host which greets a king. Round the point of the harbour, with flags flying and drums beating, came the fleet of Karika. " Be of good cheer, Tangiia," he cried across the water, "for I am coming." So Tangiia gained new heart. " Fight on," he cried to his men, " for Karika is with us." Then how they fought the enemy in front, and how Karika bore down upon them in the rear, you would need the men of Raratonga to tell you, for I cannot do the battle justice. Tutabu was beaten, half of his canoes wrecked, many of his bravest warriors killed, and he, with the miserable remnant, fled for dear life over the sea, where Karika still allowed him to wander for a little while, a miserable outcast on the face of the earth.

If you ask the Raratongans where Tangiia and Karika are now, they will tell you that they went away lorg ages ago to Bolotoo, the beautiful island in the far north-west, where the brave and good dwell in happiness forever. Tangiia became an old man on Raratonga, but never again did Tutabu come to take him. One day he saw the doves of beautiful plumage. They bore a vessel on their outstretched wings, grander than that which had borne him from Tahiti. And lo ! in that vessel, when it touched the water, Tangiia beheld his king, Taaroa, in all his princely glory, but when he spoke the voice was Karika's. " Come home," he said. So Tangiia stepped into the royal canoe and, upborne by the doves, it swam through the balmy air far into the north-west sea and landed at Bolotoo, whose shores no mortal ever saw, whose joys no mortal tongue can tell. But the doves and the canoe and Karika too, dim in outline, yet very real, are ever coming from the island of the blessed to other isles and lands north and south, east and west, to take the brave and the good home to the place where the wicked cease from troubling and the weary are at rest.

What does this story teach us ? It tells us the old Bible story, repeated in so many forms in the traditions of the world, of sin coming to our earth in the disobedience of the first man. It agrees with that story in showing that there was sin in the great universe of God before man fell, and in pointing to him who tempted man as his greatest enemy. But it tells us something for ourselves rather than for Adam and other people. It shews us to ourselves as disobedient children of the God of holiness and love. We know that God is angry with us for our sins, so that we do not see Him

near, and do not dare to seek Him.   But we do not want to
be ruled over by the great deceiver, for we have sense
enough to see that his wages are death.   And yet we never
could get away from his power if God's ship did not come to
our help, if the Holy Spirit, the true heavenly dove, did not
come to us and place us in the boat of Christian education,
with the paddles of good resolves and the sails of better
desires.   Then, as we go on our way, the enemy follows us
with sore temptations, urging us to give up all our hopes
and efforts for a truer life of liberty.   Like the canoe that
went from island to island, we go from one companionship
to another, from one occupation or kind of soul life to
another, ever hoping to be free, but ever followed and sometimes sore wounded by the great adversary.   At last we give
up our trust in all these refuges of good works, or self-
denial, or seeking to make ourselves better, and go forth on
the open sea of God's mercy.   Alas we would soon perish
there from sheer starvation of soul, if God's love had not
made a rest for us in the midst of mercy.   We see the living
things in that mercy which is over all God's works ; we behold strange monsters of other lands and dark ages finding
something there to hope in ; but as sinners we are alone
upon it, fugitives still.   Then over the waters comes the
Father in the Son, and He a man like ourselves, but a pure
holy strong man.   We are afraid, but what can we do ? He
is holy, and sin cannot dwell with holiness, nor can we
escape from that holy presence which is everywhere.   We
yield our hearts to Him and submit to his terms.   He hears
our prayer, and as we promise to be faithful He accepts us.
Then His Word comes to our help, the strong Old Testament with the holy law, the gentle New Covenant with the
blessed Gospel.   These bring us sweet rest and peace.   But

the battle is not over. The enemy of our souls will not give up his prey. He comes while we are resting and thinking ourselves safe. Temptations fall upon us suddenly, but our consciences, taught by the Word and Spirit of God, are quick. We see our danger, and with all our new found powers, reinforced by the truth of the living Word, face the enemy. As we join battle our hearts go forth in prayer, the trumpet note which calls for help and makes Satan tremble. It is answered. Christ is for us, then who can be against us? Our foes are beaten back, and we are more than conquerors through Him that loved us. The wicked one may come again and again, but we need not fear, for God's help is ever with us. We dwell in perfect peace, because our hearts are stayed on God. Some day the enemy will come no more, but in all His glory Christ will come to bear us home to the country into which sin shall never enter.

In few words the lesson of the story is this: The only deliverance from the guilt of sin on our consciences and the power of sin in our hearts and lives is found in surrendering ourselves to God by accepting the yoke of Jesus Christ, His Son.

VII.

𝕭𝖆𝖑𝖉𝖊𝖗.

●

Balder.

"Except ye be converted and become as little children, ye shall not enter into the kingdom of heaven."—Matthew xviii. 3.

Back in the golden age that lies far beyond man's memory, and in that old world from which your fathers came, was the great kingdom of Valhalla. Its king was Odin, who ruled over a goodly people in a pleasant land, for the country of Valhalla was like that which the old father of the church describes in his simple longings:

> The bitter cold or scorching heat
> Hath no admittance there ;
> The roses do not lose their leaves
> For spring lasts all the year,
> With lilies white and saffron red
> And balsam's fragrant tear."

The people, too, were strong and fair and happy as they were good, with only one exception, and that was the deceiver Loki. He also was shapely in form and regular in feature, but his mind and heart were bad. Nothing pleased him better, when he was not working some mischief himself, than to tell wicked tales of others and do all in his power to destroy the peace and harmony of the kingdom. Now, just the opposite of Loki in all respects was the beloved son of King Odin and his queen Hertha, whose name was Balder. Long ages after he had left the world, the poets never tired of singing his praises as all that was beautiful and brave and good. And even now, in the northern land where once was the kingdom of our story, the very children call the chamo-mile daisy that grows by the roadsides Balder's eyebrow, because it is the whitest living thing. His brother Thor was strong, and Bragi, eloquent, and Tyr, brave as a lion. But Balder was full of majesty and kindness, and the glance of his eye was bright and shining as the sun. So the people called him Balder the beautiful and Balder the good.

One day the royal company were assembled in the great hall of Valhalla. Odin saw that his son's face wore a slight shade of sadness, and asked Balder what it was that troubled him, since never before had he seen any trace of pain in his look. Then Balder answered that there was evil in the kingdom, and he knew that soon he would suffer from it, even to death. All in the court were greatly moved by what Balder said, but they did not believe it could be true, for they exclaimed, "Who in all the world would hurt Balder!" Still his mother Hertha thought she would make perfectly sure, and sent out a proclamation to all things living or dead in earth or air or water, that they should not harm her son. All things living and dead, the beasts of the field and the birds of the air and the fish of the sea, with rocks and trees and flowers, promised, each in its own way, that they would obey the command of their great mother and do her son no injury. Thereupon there was great joy in all hearts but that of the wicked Loki.

Nothing could hurt Balder. When a blow was aimed at him with a sharp battle-axe, his glance turned it aside ; great oaken beams shivered, and stones broke into fragments, before they touched the beloved son of Odin. All things loved him as well as all persons, so worthy was he to be loved. Now, this grieved Loki sorely. He gave himself no rest, but went everywhere throughout the kingdom, asking every-body and everything if they had promised not to hurt Balder. In earth and sea and air all answered yes. But one day he came to an oak forest and there, growing out of a tree, he saw a sickly plant of yellowish green with white waxy berries, which we now call the mistletoe ; and it seems that this plant had either not heard Hertha's proclamation, or, if it had heard, did not heed it, because it grew neither out of the earth, nor in the sea, nor in the air, but on an oak. So the mistletoe had not sworn to do no harm to Balder. Then Loki was glad. He took the mistletoe and carried it carefully hidden to the place where Balder was among his brothers and the great ones of his father's court. As they were just then striking Balder with objects of metal and wood and stone, not with the thought of doing him hurt, but of seeing with their own eyes how all things loved him, Loki came up to one of the beautiful prince's brothers, the blind Hodur, who stood apart from the rest, and asked him why he did not join in the strange contest. " I cannot see my brother," he answered, " and even if I could I have nothing to throw that I am sure might not do him harm." " Take this tender plant," replied the tempter ; "it cannot injure him, and I will guide your hand." So blind Hodur held the sprig of mistletoe in his hand, and threw it with all his might, while Loki guided his aim. It struck him full on the heart and Balder fell to the ground, dead. The sprig of mistletoe, weak, insignificant looking plant as it was, had killed him, for besides Loki, it was his only enemy. And Hodur, poor blind Hodur, through ignorance he had done the deed which plunged all Valhalla in mourning. He had trusted Loki and Loki had deceived him, as he well might have known.

9

Amid universal wailing they carried away the dead body of him who had been their pride and glory, and laid it in the great hall over night.   In the morning it was gone.

Then came a change over all Valhalla.   Odin's throne was missing, and, though his voice was heard in the air, neither he nor his beloved son were seen more.   The skies that had been ever serene and bright were now dark with a pall of clouds; the lightning shot from out them and scorched the earth with sheets of flame; and the roll of thunder upon thunder struck terror to the bravest heart. When the storm was past and the cold northern light took the place of the genial warmth of other days, it revealed a scene of desolation.   The peaceful streams had become roaring torrents ; the once calm slumbering ocean raved in madness against rough granite cliffs; smiling meadows and fruitful orchards and banks of many coloured flowers had given place to barren wastes and gloomy pine forests.   And amid all this, strange sounds were heard, the groan of pain, and the sigh of sorrow, and the wail of mourners weeping for their dead.   But above all these sad sounds arose the cry of Mother Hertha : " My Balder, my Balder, O give me back my son !"   Once more she sent out a proclamation through all the desolated land saying, " Whoever brings Balder back again shall be loved by me better than all the world beside." Yet no answer came, for the journey was one full of fear and gloom, through dark and dangerous ways, where enemies lurked that were not of flesh and blood to be met with human weapons, but ghostly and terrible beings of another world. Strong Thor would not go, giant-slayer though he was ; nor brave Tyr, that had never shrunk before an enemy ; nor clever Bragi, who knew how to win the hearts of men. Hertha prayed them all by the gloom and desolation of

Valhalla, by the love they bore her, by the joy of seeing
Balder back, to undertake the journey, but they would not.
They said it was useless to try.

> " For the beautiful is gone for ever;
> Never comes the beautiful again."

At last Balder's youngest brother, a modest young knight
named Hermoder, yielded to his mother's entreaties, and
prepared to set forth upon the dangerous errand. " If
Balder is to be found" he said, " I will find him ; if he is to
be brought back again I will bring him or perish."

A great company met with his mother Hertha to see
Hermoder on his way. As he sat full armed upon his horse
there were many that wished him well, saying " He has
something of Balder's look." But others pitied him for his
fool's errand, as they called it, and others mocked, and Loki
went on before to put all kinds of stumbling blocks in his
way, for of all things he dreaded the worst was Balder's
return. Soon Hermoder left the kingdom of Valhalla behind
him as he galloped onwards with only one thought, that of
seeing his brother and bringing him back. He heard the
voice of the Allfather in the air, leading him in the way he
ought to go, and every tree by the wayside seemed to point
like a finger-post in the same direction. He was in a strange
land now, at first beautiful though weird, and then gloomy
and terrifying. Down the dark gulphs, along a narrow
bridle path on a ledge of rock, with fathomless depths beneath
him and no light of heaven but frowning cliffs towering
above, he rode, while loose stones struck against his horse's
hoofs and, falling into the abyss, seemed to utter a mocking
cry which was answered by great bat-like figures flitting to
and fro in the gloom before his eyes. Many a time he
shuddered and almost despaired. Then he would pray

" Allfather, guide thy son ; Balder, help thy brother who
seeks thee ;" and he would see a gleam of light before which
the phantoms fled, and hear above him a comforting voice.
Soon he found by his horse's pace that he was ascending,
slowly climbing upwards towards the light of day.   At
length he reached a wide plain where the way was clear, but
it was barred off from the narrow mountain pass by a great
gate, strong and high.   Behind the gate a porter sat, a
venerable man, with key in hand.   Hermoder smote the
gate with his sword, calling aloud to the porter to open
quickly for his business needed haste.

The porter answered " I will indeed open the gate, but
you must first dismount, for there is no room for your horse
to enter, nor can he enter here."   Hermoder was angry,
because the brave steed had borne him all the way from
Valhalla through danger and thick darkness, and to leave
him now, when the light shone and the way was clear,
seemed base ingratitude.   Moreover he was accustomed to
ride as became a knight of high degree, and did not care to
trudge along like a common man at arms.   So he backed
his horse to leaping distance from the gate and reined him up
for the vault that was to clear it.   A moment later and he
lay beside his horse stunned and bruised upon the ground,
for the gate was such as no power on earth could overleap.
Being thus dismounted by his own folly, and his steed not
being in condition to serve him, he rose with difficulty and
knocked once more.   Then the aged porter gladly opened a
door within the gate and welcomed Hermoder to another
stage of his journey.   And he on foot with sword and shield
walked rapidly across the plain.   Well was it for him that
his horse had not been permitted to enter, since many a pit-
fall, artfully concealed beneath the level ground, made him-

self stumble and fall, that would have been the death of horse
and rider.   He was in the light of day now, but it was a
cheerless day.   He knew the sun was shining but he could
not see its welcome face ; only in the far-off distance towards
which he was moving did he catch a gleam of mellow gold
ere it seemed to fade away.   He stumbled often as he
pressed forward more eager than his steps, for he was ill-
used to long foot marches, and his stumbles hurt him sorely,
because of the bruises he had got in his fall.   Still he kept
up his brave heart, ever and anon saying to himself, " I will
find Balder, I will bring him back again."

When the night began to fall, Hermoder's path lay through
a wood and out of it wild beasts came, some rushing open-
mouthed to meet him, others snapping at him as he passed
by, and others snarling and growling angrily at his heels.
But they did him no harm, for those that did not fall by his
sword broke their teeth and tore their claws upon his polished steel armour.   Again Hermoder thought how well it
was that he had parted with his horse, for certainly these
wild beasts would have devoured him, but he rejoiced that
he had not laid aside his heavy armour and his good sword
that had been his safety.   He had been cast down all day,
but now his heart was lifted up again, as he marched proudly
forward like a soldier who goes to battle.   In this way he
came to a high wall that ran right and left as far as the eye
could reach, and just before him in the wall he spied a narrow door.   Impatiently he knocked at the door with his
sword hilt, and when a grave voice asked " Who is there ?"
he replied " Open quickly, it is I, Hermoder, a king's son."
But the warder would not open.   He said, " This country
belongs to the great king, the king of kings, and no princes
but those of his royal house may enter here."   Then, an-

swered Hermoder humbly, " Let me in as a poor traveller
who seeks his lost brother;" and he took the helmet with its
circle of gold, which was a prince's coronet, off his head and
laid it upon the ground. " Who do you seek?" inquired
the porter. " What is your brother's name?" His name
is Balder, the beautiful and the good," replied Hermoder.
" If it be Balder you seek," said the old man, " pass on in
the king's name." So he opened the door and Hermoder,
bare-headed, without helmet or crown, entered into a new
world.

It was night, a beautiful summer night. He could not
tell what the earth was like for it was full of shadow, and he
could only see the moonbeams lying upon the ground and
thousands of stars reflected in the water. Nor did he fret
because his crown was gone, since the light from heaven
gilded the meanest things with a far brighter glory than
shone from its golden circle and precious stones. It seemed
to lift him up, that moonlit night. He felt as if he were
walking among the stars and listening to their heavenly
music. He forgot that he was a king's son and a soldier,
that he was armed with sword and shield, that he had conquered wild beasts and had travelled far from home through
many perils. He thought of Balder, and felt sure that he
would find his lost brother in some such scene of quiet
splendour as that which reigned above and won his eye
heavenward. Never could he have thrown his head back to
fix his gaze upon the skies had he worn his heavy helmet
with visor over his eyes and neckpiece pressing upon his
shoulders. This stage of his journey passed all too soon,
for, almost before he knew where he was, he heard the busy
hum of a large city where people were awaking to the business of the day, and straight before him were the city walls.

The bright sun was rising over it, but between the sun and the city was a thin yet dark cloud of vapour and smoke such as you have seen lying over manufacturing towns on a still day.

Hermoder knocked gently for admission within the city's gate. He knocked hesitatingly even, for he felt that he would far rather have been back in the night scene from which he had come. The warder waited till he knocked more boldly, and this he soon did, for he remembered that he was in search of Balder and must press forward. Then, said the porter, " Are you prepared to serve the king of this city, for none can enter here who will not serve ! " I am a soldier," he replied, "and will serve the king with my sword." " No swords can enter here," answered the warder, "·for our king will not be served with weapons of death." " Then," said Hermoder, " I will leave my sword outside the city walls, and serve your king in the way that is most pleasing." So he left his sword and shield behind him, and empty handed passed within the city walls. What a strange sight met his eyes. The city was full of people, and all that walked were burden bearers, and most of their burdens were men and women and children like themselves. Even some of these burdens carried burdens upon their shoulders or clasped in their arms, and all who did so seemed happy. " Give me some work to do for the king,'' asked Hermoder of the porter, but he answered " I have none to give ; go forward and you will find enough to do." Then Hermoder walked on, and, as he went, lamented that he was so idle when all others were busy, until he came to a street corner where a child lay in rags, helpless and wasted with disease. The pitiful look of the child won his brave heart, so that he forgot all about the duty commanded, and thought only of the little one's sad case. How glad he was that he was not encumbered with sword and shield, but that his arms and hands were free to carry the child. Tenderly he carried the little one for a long space, soothing it in his noble winning way, till a dark man with a kindly face took his burden from him and vanished away. Other burdens he bore after this, a sad, homeless woman, and a disagreeable old man, whom nobody else would be troubled to carry. And all the time he grew stronger and his burden seemed lighter, while his heart was happier. But how poor and weak he felt himself when he saw small and feeble looking people carrying great loads, such as he felt he could never lift, of whole houses and great assemblies.

At length he came to the wall at the opposite end of the city, and beyond it he could see that another city lay. The gate which led out of the one into the other was locked, but his knock made it fly open. The porter looked at him with astonishment, and said, " Is it possible that you have borne burdens in that heavy suit of armour? You must wear it no longer, but face work and peril as you are." Hermoder was sad at heart, for he was ashamed to appear among men in the plain simple dress he wore beneath his shining mail. Yet he obeyed, for he had found how right were all the other commands he had received. Stripping himself of his steel covering, he passed on his way. At first he felt so much lightened by the removal of his armour that he was prepared to carry great loads and run swiftly forward in search of his lost brother. But soon he found the way very rough for his almost naked feet, and the loads he carried wounded him sorely because he had no protection on his shoulders. Evil men mocked him and made him so angry that often his burden would fall while he went out of his way to chastise them. He had braved the wild beasts of the forest, but here the very insects stung him and the wretched city curs barked at him and snapped at his heels, till he felt ashamed of himself and wondered if he were indeed Hermoder and had any right to go in search of Balder the beautiful and the good. Then he heard the Allfather's voice in the air saying " Faint not ; be not discouraged," and this cheered him for a little time. Yet matters appeared to grow worse instead of better. Everybody and everything seemed to be his enemy. He stumbled over the stones, was bitten by the dogs, was jostled into the gutters by the crowd. His clothes were soiled and torn, his feet were blistered and sore, his flesh pricked and bleeding, his head fevered with the heat, and his heart faint and failing. Those that mocked Hermoder as he wearily dragged himself along thought very little of the king's son, but they did not know that he thought far less of himself. He called himself a poor, wretched, helpless man, and prayed the Allfather and his brother Balder to come to his help. Sometimes he thought it would be better if he were asleep in Mother Hertha's arms, with Balder all forgotten. But the Allfather kept up his heart though he did not know it, and Balder sent a gleam of light before his eyes that reminded him of the starry heavens.

A miserable sight Hermoder was as he passed out into the open country, resolved to find Balder even in his rags. Away from the city's smoke and dust, into the green fields and along the pleasant lanes, he saw the bright sun shining. Everything around him was beautiful and full of happy life and song. So long as he kept his eyes upon this fair world he was glad, but when he looked away from it upon himself his heart was full of fear and of burning shame. " They will never let me in to Balder's presence," he said ; " they will drive me like a beggar from the door." Then a sweet-voiced bird would sing a joyous note and take his thought away from self; or a lovely floweret would spring up at his feet and force his eye to dwell upon it. So lamenting his own sad state and admiring the beauty that was everywhere around him, he hastened forward between hope and fear to find him whom he loved.

At last a glorious vision met his eye; he saw the golden city. Not far away it appeared, a place of beauty such as no tongue on earth could describe nor pencil picture. In the midst of it a light shone brighter than all the rest, and there he knew must be Balder. O what longing he had to be there, what fears that he would not be allowed to enter! He heard the city's songs; his ear caught the great All-father's voice, that sounded so like Balder's; the very fragrance of the city's perfumes was wafted to him through the pure, bright atmosphere. He thought of the cities he had come through and the wondrous contrast of this. "Surely nothing that is not pure and clean can enter there," he said to himself, "and if that be so, what hope is there for me?" Yet for all that he ran forward till his way was barred by a wide, deep, swiftly-flowing river, whose opposite bank was just below the open gate of the golden city. There was an old man on the near bank like those who kept the gates through which Hermoder had passed, and not far from him in the stream lay a ferryboat. Hermoder gently and eagerly prayed the old man to take him over to the other shore, but the ferryman, if ferryman he were, refused, saying that the ferry was only for little children, for whom the Allfather had built that city of gold. "What shall I do?" asked Hermoder imploringly, "for I must find Balder my brother." "Cast yourself into the river and swim over," the old man replied ; "there is no other way." Hermoder hesitated. He could not swim that broad rapid stream in his ragged clothes, yet how could he part with them? How would he dare unclothed to enter the city and meet his brother ; how even appear before this aged man on the river bank? So he tried to draw his rags more closely around him until the old man smiled and said " You have parted with so much at the king's command, why not part with these? Are you proud of them?" Hermoder answered, " I am ashamed of them, but they are all I have ; how can I go unclothed into the king's city?" "The king has new raiment for his people," he replied ; "he that will put on new clothing must first put off the old."

Hermoder feared and trembled greatly. He could not meet Balder as a knight ; he dared not meet him as a beggar. Yet would it not be more shameless to meet him all unclad? Then on the other hand, the old man's words sank into his heart and he knew that Balder loved him, and the great Allfather too. So conquering his fear, he hastily tore away his rags and plunged into the river, striking out boldly for the other shore. The current was strong and the wind was against it ; great waves tossed him to and fro and made him their sport, till all his strength was gone. He could only cry " Help me, save me, I can do nothing !" Then he remembered no more, till the same waves lifted him up and laid him gently upon the river bank below the open gates of the golden city, and lo ! he was no longer the strong knight Hermoder, but a little babe whose pure heart knows no shame.

The officers whose duty it was to care for the little children carried the helpless Hermoder into the city and laid him down in Balder's arms, and the glorious sun-god, the beautiful and the good, clasped the infant brother in his loving embrace. What a meeting was that for Hermoder! What wealth of love he found coming out of his very help-lessness! He felt as if he could gladly lie in his brother's arms forever. But he did not forget his mother's message, and his mother's grief. " Balder, my brother," he said, " your mother weeps for you, and the old kingdom is full of gloom and pain and evil since you went away. Come back, Bal-der, and cheer our hearts ; come back and make all light again." Then Balder answered, " Many changes must there be before I come back again, and till then you must bid them come here to me. This will be your message to take to mother Hertha from her first-born son." After this Balder looked into his infant brother's face till it shone with a beauty like his own, and then gave him to the officers to carry across the river. The ferry-boat was on the bank waiting for the child, but the officers, never heed-ing, cast him into the river. Hermoder, with a brave man's heart, full of joy and hope, though but a little child, breasted the waves and swam over the tide that before had wearied him almost to death, gaining strength as he neared the shore. And now he lands, no infant but a strong man again, and there are the officers awaiting him. They clothe him in a new robe of dazzling whiteness, and fasten it round his waist with a golden girdle, and put sandals upon his feet. Then they wish him a good journey in the great king's name, and Hermoder goes forward through the pleasant country towards the City of Trials.

He came at last to the city, and its gates flew open before him. The insects buzzed around him as before, but now they could not sting. The surly, snapping curs slunk away at his approach, and when the foolish boys and wicked men threw mud at him from a distance it did not so much as leave a stain on his white robe. His sandals saved his feet among the sharp pointed stones, and even the sun had lost all power to smite, so bright was the glory that Balder had put upon his brother's head. So he came at length to the gate which led into the City of Burdens, and when it opened to him there stood in the entrance three officers of the great king with armour in their hands. It looked like his old armour in shape, but that was all; for steel there was silver, and for brass there was gold, and where a little gold and silver had been before there were gems of purest water and richest price. When his armour was fastened upon him he went to look for burdens; and what burdens he carried now! They were great loads, such as he had envied bearers before, but they were more than this. Other people might not know, but he did; they were kings' sons and kings' daughters whom he bore along the way with firm joyous step and strong embracing arm. At length he came to the place where he must lay his burden down, and pass out of city life into the quiet peaceful night.

Again the gate flew open and again the King's officers appeared. They gave him, instead of the old arms he had left without the walls, a shield so bright and shining that his eyes could hardly rest upon its face, polished like a mirror, and they placed in his hands a mighty two edged sword, so sharp that iron would not turn its point nor blunt its blade. Then he went on into the summer night as one sinks away into a beautiful dream, while the stars were the heavenly choir that sang sweet songs of the golden city, and the moonbeams on his cheek were the kisses of Balder, his brother. Alas, the day came all too soon, for he dreaded

the gloomy forest with its wild beasts and the dreary plain
with its pit-falls that lay beyond.   At the gate the warder
gave him back his helmet and crown, and yet it was not his,
but a king's crown instead of wondrous beauty and cunning workmanship, that hid the helmet from view.   He
bowed low before him, that ancient warder who had refused to let the king's son in before, for he saw by his arms
and by the glory in his face that Hermoder had come from
the golden city.   Then Hermoder went on his way fearing,
but soon his fears were turned to joy, for all things seems
to have been made new.   The cloudy pall, which had covered the sky and hidden the sunlight, had rolled away, and
the forest was no longer a dark and dismal haunt of wild
beasts, but a place of green arching avenues and grassy
paths, all bright and fragrant with opening flowers, where
the gold-green lizards sported among the ferns, and gorgeous butterflies sucked the hawthorn blossoms, and sweet-
voiced birds filled the air with melody.   And when evening
came and he passed out of the woodland into the open
plain, he found himself in the midst of waving cornfields
and fruitful orchards and verdant meadows sloping down to
meet laughing, silvery streams.   So he arrived at the place
where he had met with his great fall and left his wounded
horse behind.   He saluted the old porter kindly, who replied
with a deep reverence, and then he stood without the gate
and gazed upon its height which towered so far above him
up towards the clouds.   And he said, " Is it possible that
I, Hermoder, was ever so madly proud and foolish as to
tempt so great a leap ?"   The thought made him hang his
head in shame, when a joyous neigh fell upon his ear, and
soon after a horse's head was on his shoulder.   It was his
brave steed that he had left to die in his anxiety to find his

brother, now strong and well, with glossy coat and nostrils full of fire, and decked with royal trappings. So Hermoder's heart was lifted up once more with a tranquil, thankful confidence as he leaped into the saddle and made towards the regions of gloom.

Down the narrow path he rode, where there was but room for his horse's feet, and where, save along that path, the thickest darkness reigned. It was to him now a place of awe and wonder, but not of terror. Darkness without end was over his head ; darkness without end lay down beneath his feet. To strike against the rocky wall, to take a false step on the narrow paths, was to plunge into the fathomless abyss below. But Hermoder did not fear, for instead of the phantom flitting forms he had seen when first he rode through the depths, he now beheld white-robed silent attendants who held his good steed's bridle and hovered over the precipice close by his side. Now and again the horses' hoofs would strike loose stones on the path and spurn them into the awful darkness below, but this time their voice was not of mockery ; it was an ever deepening tone of solemn majestic praise. Now he rises up the heights, the light becoming more and more distinct. He stands on level ground again in a large, broad place and sees far off in the distance the desolated land of Valhalla.

He comes to the borders of his native country and finds the children at their play. They see him and run half affrighted towards their homes, crying all the way, " It is Balder ; he has come back again, and we have seen him !" The old people come to their doors and, as Hermoder rides by in his radiant beauty, they are deceived like the children and fall on their knees to give thanks for Balder found. Loki, beside himself with rage, rushes to meet his great enemy with

the mistletoe branch in his hand, but with one stroke of
his good sword Hermoder smites the hand that holds it from
the traitor's body and drives him howling with pain along the
road.   Mother Hertha has heard the cry, " Balder is back
again " ; and, her heart almost breaking with joy, hastens to
receive her son.   She sees the glory in Hermoder's face, the
royal crown, the kingly garb ; she does not doubt that her lost
son is found.   But where is brave Hermoder ? He leaps from
his horse and kneels at his mother's feet.   " I am not Balder,"
he says ; " I am only your youngest son Hermoder, but I
have seen Balder ; I have a message from him to you, and
now I plead with you in Balder's name to hear his words and
do his loving will."

Mother Hertha called her sons and her court and all her
people together in the desolate hall of Valhalla, to listen to
Balder's message.   Loki, howling with rage and pain, stopped
many on their way by saying that Hermoder's words were
lies, that he had not seen Balder, that he was trying to win
their affections and take Balder's place as their ruler.   Some
believed him, and went back to their gloomy homes ; but
others knew him for a liar and went forward to the meeting
place.   Then Hermoder told his story, how he went to find
Balder, and after many trials found him, King in the Golden
City : and how Balder told him to take to Mother Hertha
and to them all this message from her first born son.   " Many
changes there must be before I come again, but till then come
you here to me." He told them of the city, of Balder's love :
he told them of the way with all its labours and perils, and
offered to be their guide.   His face shone with Balder's
glory while he told his tale, and many believed his words
because of what they saw.   Poor blind Hodur, though he
did not see, believed, and cried out in the assembly, " Let

me go; lead me to Balder if he will take me in." Then Hermoder, strong and brave and confident, took his blind brother who had done the great wrong, and brought him safely through all the labours and dangers of the way to Balder in the Golden City. Thither went strong Thor and clever Bragi, and brave Tyr, and thousands more of young and old, all but Mother Hertha, who waits till Balder comes, when she, too, will be taken home. And when they came to the great river's bank, all the little children who had not lost their childhood went over in the ferry straight to Balder's throne and to his loving arms, but all the others had to throw away their rags and swim the stream and be cast up help-less babes upon the silver sands on the other side, where the King's messenger carried them into the City of Gold.

———

Balder, the white, though nothing more in old world story than one of the gods of a cruel pagan system, may fitly be made a type of the pure Son of God, in whom men have seen the Father. By man's ignorant yielding to the tempter in an act of disobedience, His glory was taken from earth, and by man He was even crucified and slain. The earth misses its Lord. The whole creation groaneth and travaileth in pain, waiting for His appearing, when its youth and beauty shall be restored. Man, who is the crown of that creation, hears the many voices of the world's wailing, and goes forth to seek Him whose loss it mourns. He goes to seek his brother, divine and glorious, but human, too; that he may bring Him to rule on earth as He rules in heaven. He goes armed and equipped with all earth's panoply, with strong will and high philosophy, with lofty and exclusive pride of purpose, with a fancied spotless life and great faith in self. But the

10

way to Chrisf lies through fathomless depths of sin, into which He himself descended, over a lofty wall which shuts that sin out from the distant approaches of the holy city, the wall of God's holiness which none can overleap; through a region of snares and temptations where many a fall teaches human weakness; through fields of hard Christain labour in bearing other's burdens; and through scenes of sore trial and temptation. But whether the Christ seeker's path leads through all of these or not, he loses little by little all his human armour and adornment, and all helpless, unarmed and unclad, he casts himself upon the tide of God's great love that encircles the world. Then he finds Christ and learns that He cannot return to reign till the time of the restitution of all things. Back into the world he comes to tell the story of what he has seen and heard, and, as he returns, for everything he cast away he gets a better; stronger will, and nobler learning, purer purpose, holier life, and trust in God. Thus the glory of Christ rests upon him, so that men take knowledge of him that he has been with Jesus, and, listening to the message of one who knows, themselves press into the heavenly kingdom.

Happy are you, boys and girls, if you can but keep the little child's spirit of humility and confidence in seeking your Saviour, and thus have little you have learned to love and trust to cast away on your pilgrimage to God's rest.

VIII.

The Treasure-Seeker.

VIII.

The Treasure-Seeker.

" Neither shall they say, ' Lo here ! or Lo there !' for behold
the kingdom of God is within you."—Luke xvii. 21.

The glory of Babylon had departed. That great city,
over which the proud king Nebuchadnezzar once ruled,
and by whose rivers and canals the captive Jews sat down
to weep over the destruction of Jerusalem, had become a
mere village in the desert. The walls, which once surrounded so much life and activity, so much wealth and
luxury, pomp and state, were now an enclosure for wild
beasts. Great trees grew out of its palaces, and the streets,
that in old days were busy with the hum of many thousand
voices and with the tread of many thousand feet, were all
overgrown with thickets of thorny shrubs overrun by
creeping vines. Yet in the village, by the side of the
deserted walls which still bore the name of Babylon, there
were many signs of life. Wise Jews dwelt there who spent
their time chiefly in studying the Old Testament writings,
that they might keep them pure, and free them from the
mistakes which ignorant or careless scribes had allowed to
creep into their copies of the sacred books. There also
lived some heathen philosophers, if they deserved that
name, who thought, because Babylon in the ancient times
had been a great school of magical science, that it would
help their studies if they followed them near its ruins. And

there too were a few merchants who traded into the west with the rich wares of Persia and India, and carried into these eastern lands the fabrics of Egypt and Syria, of Asia Minor and the distant continent of Europe.

Among these merchants who had grown very rich by attention to business, was one Elgnathir, the father of an only son, whose name was Yoreth. Nobody knew how rich Elgnathir was. He lived in princely style with many attendants, and his son Yoreth was brought up as it became the heir of great possessions. But the merchant owned no land save that on which his house was built, and in that house there were no treasuries with strong doors shutting up his stores of silver and gold. Often in the dead of night, when Elgnathir and his son were peacefully sleeping, the robbers from the desert would enter some other part of the great house quietly and search on every side for the place in which the merchant's treasures lay. But they never found them, and had to leave with nothing better perhaps than a silver cup or costly dress which chanced to be lying in some chamber, and which the rich trader hardly missed. Yet he always had wealth enough to live in a way that made all the neighbours envy him, and to give abundantly to the poor and those who were worthy of his aid. Sometimes Yoreth would ask his father where he kept his treasures, but Elgnathir only answered that he would know soon enough, and in the meanwhile it was better to be sure that the wealth was his than to know where it was kept. Hardly a day passed that many persons, and sometimes large companies in caravans, did not come to the merchant's house with money and other valuable things for him, so that Yoreth and the neighbours began to think they were his messengers, bringing from time to time what was needed for daily outlay from some distant and secret hiding place.

There was one man who was supposed to know where the merchant's treasures lay. At least so everybody said, however true it may have been. His name was Abdallah, and he was the most trusted and beloved of all Elgnathir's servants. He had been carried away from Arabia a slave, and the merchant of Babylon had bought him. Then, because he was a faithful youth, and especially because he loved his son with more than a brother's love, the good old trader advanced him to high honour, and set him over all his household. Next to his father Yoreth loved Abdallah, for he was wise enough to see that this trusted servant thought only of what was for his good, and generous enough to return the love which he felt for his master's son. Often did the father speak to Abdallah about his boy, and as often did Abdallah promise that he would watch over him and do all things that Elgnathir commanded him to do for the young heir. So Yoreth grew up to manhood, leading a happy life in the Babylonian village. He learned much about the living creatures in the woods and on the plains; how to manage his horse and ride in the chase; to swim in the great river and lure the fish out of its watery depths. He learned something too, from the ruins and the stories of the wise men, about the great city of ancient days under the shadow of whose walls he lived; and many a piece of sculptured stone, and clay tablet covered with strange letters shaped like arrowheads, found its way into his cabinet of curiosities. His father spoke Greek and Arabic and Syriac, and all these languages the young Yoreth picked up, just as we in childhood picked up our English tongue, so that he could talk as well in the one as in the others. From Abdallah, who had travelled far in his father's service, he learnt other languages, the Persian 'near home,' and the stately Latin of the far west. And the pious Jews, working away with their manuscripts of the Bible, were only too glad to find in the merchant's son a student of that ancient Hebrew speech which they believed to be the oldest in the world.

With the knowledge of all these languages Yoreth was able to talk with the traders and other travellers who came to visit his father or explore the ruins of Babylon. He learnt from them the history of the lands from which they came. They described the magnificence of Ecbatana and Ctesiphon, the capitals of the great Persian kings; the silent majesty of Jerusalem; the new glories of Constantinople; and the wonders of the seven-hilled Rome, once mistress of all the world. He longed to see himself the scenes which they described, and wondered greatly if his father's treasures came from any of these great seats of wealth and splendour. His father had brought him up as a Christian to believe in the only true God and in the Lord Jesus Christ whom He had sent, but Yoreth found there were people in the world who had not the same faith. He was well acquainted with many Jews to whom Jerusalem was very dear, but who hated to hear the holy name of that blessed Saviour who had trod its unworthy streets. Persians too he had met, learned, kindly, and as far as he could see, honest and faithful men, who yet worshipped the Sun and knew nothing of the great story of man's redemption. And it seemed strange to him to hear from western travellers that there were many thousands of people in the world who never tried to find out the truth about God and the world to come, but believed, or pretended to believe, whatever they were commanded by emperor or priest.

At last a sad day came to Yoreth. His father lay upon his death-bed. Suddenly the good merchant had been stricken down, and now all his friends and servants who were near stood around his couch to hear his dying words. Elgnathir had a kind word and a good word for everyone, and bestowed many gifts upon them. Then, when all were gone except his son and Abdallah, who wept sorely to lose a loving father and kind master and friend, he left to Yoreth his house and all that it contained, together with his great store of hidden wealth "which" he said, "Abdallah will tell you about." After this he breathed his last, and Yoreth and Abdallah were left alone. The time of lying-in-state passed away; the sad and solemn funeral, attended by hundreds of mourners of every nation, took place; the days of mourning were accomplished, and Yoreth lifted up his tearful eyes to become lord over the household in his father's place. Those who had mourned at the funeral came into the young lord's presence, saying, "Elgnathir, the noble, the generous, the good, has been gathered to his fathers; long may his son, Yoreth, follow in his steps." And as it was the last day of the year, they wished him all prosperity and happiness in the year that was to come. When they were alone, Abdallah said to Yoreth "Let us now find your father's will and see where the great treasures are that he has left to you." But Yoreth replied "No, not to-day; it is too soon after the time of mourning; let us wait at least until the new year dawns. To-morrow is time enough to look for the treasures. We have plenty in the house to last us for many a long day." Abdallah pressed his young master only to look at the instructions his father had left, but, finding his entreaties to be useless, he ceased; and so the last day of the year passed away.

It was late on New Year's day when Yoreth awoke, for heart and eyes were still heavy with grief. Abdallah put into his hands a silver casket, in the lock of which he had placed a golden key. Yoreth turned the lock, and, when the little box was opened, found a piece of parchment folded up within it and nothing more. He took the parchment out, unfolded it, and read what was written upon it in the Syrian tongue. It said, " I leave all my great wealth to my only son and heir Yoreth. He will find this wealth in the city of the great King. In the centre of that city stands a palace, and, in the middle of that palace, a courtyard. In the midst of the courtyard lies a stone, and beneath that stone the treasure rests. Let him look there at the moment that the old year passes into the new, and he will be the richest man in the world." When Abdallah heard this he wept because the hour spoken of in the writing was long passed and another year must end before the treasure could be found. But he said to Yoreth, " Let us begin at once and make preparations for next New Year's morning. Yoreth seemed sorry that that the time had gone by, but he answered, " What does it matter, since we do not know where the city of the Great King is ? We would not have had time to find it, but now we have abundance of time to make enquiries and be sure that we are seeking in the right way." So he went out into the village and spoke to the people he met about his father, and asked them questions about the city of the Great King.

When Yoreth asked in a careless way about the City of the Great King, he received careless answers suited to the thoughts of the people to whom he spoke. Those, whose fathers and grandfathers had lived under the shadow of Babylon's ruins told him that it used to be the city he wanted, but its king and glory had departed, and they knew no other. There had been a City of the Great King, but now there was none. The Jews turned their eyes to the west towards Jerusalem, and there were tears in them as they said, " Beautiful for situation, the joy of the whole earth is Mount Zion on the sides of the north, the City of the Great King." Yoreth asked a Greek merchant about the city, and he replied, " It is Constantinople, queen of the seas, that lies between two continents, the city which the great Constantine, first emperor of the Christian faith, founded to bear his royal name." Then the young man met a priest in monkish dress, who had come from the far west to visit Bible lands and write about them. " Where," he asked this venerable man, " is the City of the Great King ?" The Monk answered, " It is the City of God, the place that he has chosen as the centre of the world, from whence His holy Church is to rule all nations of men ; it is Rome where St. Paul and St. Peter taught the truth and died." The last· whom Yoreth addressed were noblemen from the court of Persia who had come to collect the Baby-lonian taxes. They laughed when he told them of the answers he had received to his questions, and said, " The Great King is our master, the Lord of Babylon and all this eastern world, and he has two great cities. One of these from whence we come is Ecbatana, his summer abode away among the Median mountains in the north ; and the other is Ctesiphon, where he spends the winter, not far away from you on the great river Tigris. Each of these is the City of the Great King."

Yoreth told Abdallah all that he had heard, and proposed that they should go as soon as possible to Ctesiphon as it was near at hand and because the great king was then living there. Abdallah asked his young master to wait a little longer and make sure of the city where the treasure lay. But Yoreth was so certain that it was either Ctesiphon or Ecbatana that he was not willing to make any more enquiries. Accordingly Abdallah collected all the money and jewels his old master had left, sold the gold and silver plate, and rented the house for a large sum to an Armenian merchant. Thus in a few days he and Yoreth were able to travel in state to the city of Ctesiphon. There, though it was winter, they found a warm delightful climate, and came out of their home of mourning and silence into a scene of life and gaiety such as the young Babylonian had never witnessed. Since he was rich and handsome, well educated and skilled in manly sports, he soon found his way into the King's court, and amid its pleasures forgot the great purpose for which he had left his home. After a month or two had passed, the warm weather of the south became insupportable; the King gave orders to move his court to his summer residence in Ecbatana, and Yoreth decided to go with the King. " Let us at least spend a year in this city," said Abdallah, " if it be the city of the Great King, or our work will not bring us what we are seeking." Yoreth would not stay. He was fast becoming self-willed, for the young Persian noblemen, with whom he spent most of his time, led him to imitate them in their headstrong race after the pleasures of the moment. Yet he condescended to reason with Abdallah and told him how much more beautiful Ecbatana was than Ctesiphon. He was sure that it was the true city of the great King and there he meant to search in real earnest.

So to Ecbatana among the mountains of Media they went in the king's train. When they reached the city, Yoreth's joy knew no bounds. "Look, Abdallah!" he cried, "did you ever in all your wanderings see anything half so beautiful?" "It is very beautiful" the servant answered with a heavy heart, but he did not say that he had often been there before, and that sometimes in the morning, when the gates were opened that had been closed since sundown, he had seen little companies of strong men and tender women and young children frozen to death upon the white but pitiless snow, on the very threshold of so much magnificence. Yoreth knew nothing of this. He could not take his eyes away from the city as it rose up the hill-side, with its seven walls standing higher as they ascended, each capped with its snowy battlements, first white, then black, next scarlet, blue, orange, and within, silver and gold. In the centre within the golden walls was the palace of the great king. Through the seven gates the royal procession passed, while the people, high and low, who came to meet it, bowed their heads in reverence, or lay upon the ground with their faces kissing the dust. Thousands of slaves were there, and many of them broken-hearted slaves, but Yoreth rode proudly in the king's train and troubled himself little with thoughts of others.

The summer months sped swiftly by in the glorious city, and in the neighbouring woods and gardens. All through that summer the roses lasted, and the songs of the birds scarce ceased by day or by night. Yoreth drank the full cup of pleasure, and, when the time came for the court to return to Ctesiphon, he was so much in love with the city on the mountain that it needed no great persuasion on the part of Abdallah to make him stay. So the king and his courtiers departed, leaving Yoreth almost alone among the officers, the merchants, and the common people who lived

there all the year round.   Soon the winter made its appearance.   The snow began to fall, and with the snow the wild
beasts came down the mountain sides and filled the parks
and gardens with danger.   The roses vanished and the song-
birds followed the court.   The snow lay upon the gaudy
battlements and hid their many-tinted beauties from the eye.
Yoreth, too, began to think.   He had spent much money
and was none the better for it ; he had given much time to
the king and his courtiers, and was none the wiser for it all.
The young Babylonian became sad.   He opened his eyes
to the wretchedness and misery of the town.   He saw the
slaves who toiled without rest, that others might be happy
through their labours and tears.   He almost fancied that the
seven great circling walls, scarlet and azure, silver and gold
though they were at the top, were all crimson beneath with
the blood of many victims on whose weary lives they had
been reared.   He despaired of finding his father's treasure
in such a city.

The old year was dying when Yoreth was in this frame of
mind.   He called Abdallah.   " Come, my faithful friend,"
he said, in tones that touched the servant's heart, " let us
seek for the treasure and make sure, though I fear much it
is not to be found in this place."   So they went together
with a measuring line and, because they knew that the gold-
capped wall was in the centre of the city, they only measured
within its bounds, to find that the king's palace lay exactly
in the middle of the area it surrounded.   The palace was
built round about a square or courtyard, and in the middle
of that courtyard was a great slab of stone on which, though
much worn, Yoreth could still trace letters, very old letters
like those he had seen on the stones of Babylon.   It was the
last day of the old year when Yoreth gained permission from

the keeper of the palace to spend the night within its walls with his faithful servant. They took in with them a heavy iron bar to lift the stone, and a strong pick to break the ground beneath. Patiently they waited under one of the corridors looking out upon the court, until they could hear a gentle hum in the city, as of people rising and preparing for something to happen. Then came a burst of sound from bells and gongs, together with the shouts of the people crying to one another, "the New Year is come !" At once they lifted the stone, heavy though it was. They broke the ground beneath it, which yielded readily and softly to their blows. Down they dug, three, four, five, six feet into the earth, but no treasure chest appeared. Abdallah brought a lamp to the pit and examined the fragments of stone and earth which had been thrown out of it. Carved marble and ivory were there, gaily coloured bricks and tiles, shreds of gold and silver plating, pieces of stone with ancient writing upon them, and sticks of wood all charred by fire. " There is nothing for us here," said Abdallah, " nothing but the ruins of an old city which once stood here, that must have been as beautiful at least in its time as that in which we stand. So some day this great city will perish and be hidden forever in the dust. Arise, Yoreth, my master, let us away to seek the City of the Creat King."

Yoreth and Abdallah filled the hole with earth again and set the stone in its place. Then they talked till daylight of where they should go. Yoreth remembered the kind-hearted Jews who had taught him Hebrew, and what they had said about Jerusalem. " Let us go there," he said, "for I have heard that people, Christian people from all parts of the world, are going there, and, certainly, it was once the City of the Great King." When daylight came they prepared for their journey, and soon were on their way. It was a very difficult and dangerous journey, across the rugged mountains which divide Media from Assyria, then over the Tigris river into Mesopotamia, and over the Euphrates into Syria. But the weather became milder and more pleasant as they advanced, and when they reached Palestine, although the roads were wet and slippery with mud, there was no snow and the spring seemed not very far away. With rejoicing they rode at last into the streets of Jerusalem, and in that city took up their home. While staying for a time at a place of public entertainment, Yoreth sought the company of learned Jews, many of whom dwelt in the city of their fathers. They were very shy of him at first because he was a Christian, but when he told them of their fellow-countrymen with whom he had conversed in Babylon, and who had taught him their ancient language, they became more friendly and asked how they could serve him. Yoreth did not tell them about the treasure, but he let them know he was seeking for the City of the Great King. Thereupon they promised, if he would accept their teaching, to prove to him beyond any doubt that that city was Jerusalem. The young Babylonian agreed and went every day to the Jews' quarter to hear them expound the Old Testament Scriptures.

A few weeks' instruction served to convince Yoreth that Jerusalem was the City of the Great King. Then he asked Abdallah how much money remained of what he had carried away from Babylon. There was not much left, but by selling some gems that had belonged to his father, enough would be made up to live upon for some time to come. Abdallah sold the gems and the sum he obtained for them was so great that Yoreth determined to buy the house in which his treasure lay, so that no one might hinder him digging for it when the time came. Together he and Abdallah went through Jerusalem, carefully taking its measurements till they found the central house. It had a courtyard, and in that courtyard was a stone. On this stone were some Hebrew letters, partly worn away, which Abdallah said meant "a law," but which Yoreth was sure meant "search." However the house was for sale, so they bought it with half their money, and at once moved into it with all they possessed. Every day Yoreth went to see the Jewish Rabbis or they came to see him in his newly bought house. They talked of nothing but the city of the Great King, and when they parted at night Yoreth would take up his own Hebrew Bible and read all the passages written by David and other holy men of old about Jerusalem. Sometimes he was astonished to find that the later Jewish writers spoke of it as a very wicked city which had been once destroyed because of its sins, but then again others said such beautiful things about it that he was re-assured and did not repent the bargain he had made.

At last the wished-for end of the year came. There was no need for stealing away silently to the place where the treasure lay, for the house was all Yoreth's own. Everything was made ready. The rabbis were invited to come and see the treasure, and, shortly before the hour of midnight, they went out with Yoreth and Abdallah and a company of servants with crowbars and spades into the courtyard. When the last grain of sand fell in the hour-glass which Abdallah held in his hand, the stone was raised and the digging began. After going down a few feet through soft earth, one of the spades struck something that gave forth a ringing sound and made Yoreth's heart leap with hopeful joy. Carefully the servants uncovered it and showed the lid of a small iron chest. "Here are the treasures!" cried Yoreth, almost beside himself with

happiness.   The men reached down and found the handles.
They lifted it up with ease, for it was very light, and when
Abdallah saw this his countenance fell, although his master
was so full of hope that he noticed nothing but the box.   A
rusty key was fastened by a chain to one of the handles.
Yoreth seized the key, broke the slight chain that held it, and
put it into the lock.   The lock turned with a harsh grating
sound.   The lid flew open and showed a roll of mouldy
leather.   " This can't be the treasure," thought Yoreth,
" but it will tell me where to find the treasure."   So the
leather case was stripped off, and then another case or wrapping of softer skin, and then appeared a scroll of parchment
covered with old Hebrew letters.   Yoreth showed the manu-
script to the oldest rabbi, who gave thanks to God and cried
" Wonderful, Wonderful ! was there ever such a treasure ;
it is the oldest writing of the cursing upon Mount Ebal I
have ever seen."   When Yoreth heard this, the blood left
his face ; for a moment he stood like a stone, speechless ;
then with a groan he staggered and would have fallen fainting to the ground if Abdallah had not caught him in his
arms.   " Keep the parchment treasure and leave us !" cried
the faithful servant to the rabbis.   So Yoreth and he were
once more alone in their sorrow.

Elgnathir's son was ill for many long days, but Abdallah
nursed him carefully and tenderly.   When he recovered, he
said to his faithful attendant, " Let us go away from this
place for I can hear nothing but the cursing of Mount Ebal.
Even the ruins of Ecbatana were not so bad as this."
" Where next shall we go ?" asked Abdallah ; and Yoreth
answered feebly, " To Constantinople, where reigns the
great Christian emperor."   A rich Jew bought the house for
more than they had paid for it, because he had heard of the

finding of the parchment scroll and hoped to discover other treasures beside. Then with what they got from the sale of the house and the little ready money which remained over, they departed to the sea coast and took ship for Constantinople. The sea voyage did the young man good, for it brought new scenes before his eyes ; the coasts of Palestine and Syria, the island of Cyprus, the southern shores of Asia Minor, the lovely Ægean sea with its many islands, the narrow Hellespont or strait of the Dardanelles, which carried the ship, like a river, into the Propontis or Sea of Marmora, and, last of all, that spacious harbour, the Golden Horn, crowded with innumerable vessels and the riches of many lands. With some regret at first Yoreth and Abdallah left the ship in which they had spent such happy days, but when they walked the streets of the city of Constantine and saw its palaces, its churches, its markets, with all their grandeur and signs of wealth, the regret disappeared and they rejoiced that at last they had found the city of the great King.

It was no easy task to find the centre of Constantinople, for the city was fourteen miles round. Many weeks passed before Yoreth and Abdallah found that a church stood in the middle of it, a church with a great domed over space in the midst, and a long flat stone on the pavement such as they had been taught to expect. How could they ever hope to get the treasure from this sacred place? Would it not be death to attempt such sacrilege? Their money too was almost gone, for it cost a great deal to live at Constantinople. Yoreth made up his mind to become a soldier, one of the emperor's guard if possible, and to get the help of some of his fellow soldiers, after he had gained their friendship and promised them rewards, to recover his father's wealth, for he did not doubt that it was lying beneath that stone. The next day he offered himself to the chief captain of the imperial guard, and as he was a handsome, tall young man and could manage a horse and his arms well, the captain bade him take the soldier's oath of fidelity to the emperor and put on his uniform. Then, after a few day's training, he was allowed to take his place in the ranks, sometimes on horseback when the emperor went abroad, and at others on foot when he mounted guard about the palace. Abdallah would not become a soldier. He said he was a man of peace and had no love for even the outward signs of war. So he engaged himself to an eastern merchant living in the city and entered anew upon a trader's life.

Yoreth became a great favourite with his new comrades. His officers also thought highly of him, and the emperor himself stopped more than once to look at the tall, handsome soldier who kept guard from time to time at the doors of his apartments. In consequence of all this the young Babylonian was promoted to the rank of a petty officer and the command of ten men, most of whom chanced, like himself, to come from the east. The time passed rapidly by, and, when the old year was near its end, Yoreth was surprised and delighted to hear that the emperor intended to visit the very church where his treasure lay upon the New Year, and that he and his guard of ten were to prepare to receive him. Already on many occasions he had accompanied the emperor to other churches and had knelt or bowed or presented arms at the service, because such were the emperor's orders, without thinking much or at all about what it meant. Now, however, he was to be in a church on business that concerned him more than the emperor or anyone else. He spoke to the soldiers under his command whom he could trust, and promised them great rewards out of his father's hidden treasure. The eve of the New Year came. Yoreth's officer called him forth and made him march his men to the church and guard all its doors, that nobody might enter save the priests until the emperor should come in the morning to join in the New Year's service. With a glad heart full of hope Yoreth marched to the centre of the city and set his guards at the doors of the sacred building.

The Roman soldier remained on guard for six hours at a time. There were only four doors to place sentries over, and over these Yoreth set men whom he could trust, because they would be relieved before the time to search came, and then he could fill their places with four who were not his friends. Midnight came. The four trusty guardsmen came in and the four doubtful ones went to their posts. The priests and acolytes had finished their preparations and retired to rest, that they might be fresh and ready for their duties on the morrow. Yoreth and his six companions hastened to the stone. With great difficulty they raised it, without looking at what was written upon its surface. Some distance below lay another stone which they loosened from its bed with their short swords, when a sickening odour that almost stifled them rose into the air. They lifted it up on end, and there, to their horror and disappointment, they saw that they had raised the lid of a great stone coffin in which lay, in faded purple robe and with a golden crown upon its head, the decaying body of an emperor. "It is the great Emperor Constantine," cried one of the soldiers; "I knew he was buried in this church, but never thought this villain here would have made us do so foul a deed." Then advancing towards the horror-stricken Yoreth, he cried, "You shall pay for this. Come comrades, seize him in the emperor's name." Then Yoreth regained his senses. He dashed the soldier who spoke to the pavement with an alarming clang of his armour on the stones, then rushed to the nearest door, overturned the sentinel who stood before it, and fled away in terror through the silent streets.

When he had run sufficiently far without meeting anyone, Yoreth slackened his pace and marched with military step towards the quarter where Abdallah lodged. Happily the faithful servant was awake, wondering what had happened to his young master and anxious for his safety. Gladly he took him in, gave him a change of clothing, and then led him down to the water side, where a vessel lay that was to set sail next morning for Italy. Abdallah easily persuaded the captain, who was carrying goods for his employer, to sail at once as the wind was blowing fair, and at the same tmie dropped Yoreth's uniform which he had brought with him into the deep harbour. Anxiously did this devoted friend stand on the shore watching the ship sail slowly away, for he could hear an alarm in the city, the sound of a trumpet, and the tramp of horsemen in the streets. Soon the vessel rounded the Horn and was lost to sight, but not a moment too soon, for the horsemen of the imperial guard came nearer, they saw him, and seized him as their prisoner. They dragged Abdallah to the light and looked at his face, only to find that he was not the man they wanted. "What are you doing here at this time of night?" they asked. "Looking for a ship that had a cargo of my employer's on board," he replied; "but it is goné and I am very glad, as it will arrive all the sooner in Italy." The horsemen took

Abdallah home, searched his house, led him to his employer and questioned him about the ship. All he had said was true, so the faithful servant was allowed to finish his night's rest in peace.

Abdallah remained in Constantinople and prospered. Yoreth in the Italian vessel arrived after some days at Portus, a town situated by the mouth of the river Tiber, and the seaport of Rome. There he landed and, borrowing a small sum of money from the captain of the ship, set out for the great city which once ruled the world. He found Rome all that he had expected, and even more than he had hoped. It was not so showy as Constantinople, nor so bright with barbaric splendour as Ecbatana, nor so beautifully situated as Jerusalem, but it was vast and solid and impressive in its ancient grandeur. There he met people of all lands and men of every occupation. Soldiers and sailors, merchants and traders, noblemen and slaves, with their wives and children, thronged the streets from morning till night. But what struck Yoreth's attention most was the great number of priests he met, walking silently along or muttering to themselves as they went, though they seemed to have little else to do. He chanced to fall in with an old acquaintance, a merchant whom he had seen in Babylon, and asked him why there were so many of these black robed people, and what they did. The merchant replied that many young men became priests because they thought it the best way to win eternal life, and that they were holy men who spent their time in the service of God. So when Yoreth's friend left him, he, thinking that these holy men must love God's children as well, went up to one of them as he walked and saluted him in good Latin. The priest muttered a few words and passed on.

Then Yoreth, thinking he had not been understood, touched
the priest's shoulder with his finger and repeated the saluta-
tion, whereupon the holy man turned sharply about and
said, to the young Babylonian's great astonishment,
" Begone fellow, and do not insult the servant of God at
his devotions." Poor Yoreth had no thought of injuring
any man; he only wanted some kind words and sympathy
of feeling. And this was all he got for his pains. " Truly,"
he said to himself; " this Rome may be the city of the
great king, but it is the home of little men."

Yoreth found rest in an inn that night, but in the morning, when he had paid his score, all his money was gone.
What could he do? He dared not send word to Abdallah,
for the Emperor at Constantinople might find out where he
was and have him arrested. Still he was determined to
find his father's treasure, and for this purpose he spent all
the day upon the streets seeking information about the
centre of the city. There were some kindly people in
Rome, and one of them, who was an architect and surveyor,
told him of an inner circle where all the great forums or
market-places and courthouses were, inside which he could
easily discover the central building. That night the young
Babylonian slept in the gateway of one of these fora, and
when he awoke, long before the city was astir, he measured
the distance by his military step, and found the building
that stood in the very middle of Rome. It was not a handsome structure, square and high, built of rough stone, and
with large numbers of little window-like openings with bars
over them. " It is very like a prison," he thought. Still
he had dared great things already for his father's treasure,
and not even a prison would stop his search. So when
daylight came in all its fullness and people began to go

about the streets, Yoreth knocked at the door of the forbidding mansion. His knock was answered by a man in a black robe with a rough girdle about his waist, and to him Yoreth made request that he might have some food as he had tasted none for a whole day, offering at the same time to do any kind of work in payment. The man answered, "We are poor priests ourselves and cannot support strong lazy beggars." Then Yoreth said, "Take me for your servant; I am strong as you say, and I am not lazy; I will serve you faithfully if you will only accept my service." "No," replied the porter, "we have had servants like you before who stay with us while it pleases them, and then they run away." "Take me for your slave then" cried Yoreth despairingly, "I will sell myself to you for nothing." On hearing this the little black eyes of the porter twinkled, and he said "Come inside the door and wait till I see what can be done." So he left him standing inside the door for a few minutes and then came back with three other priests. Finding he was still willing to be their slave, these priests drew up a form of writing which they made him sign, by which he promised to obey them in all things, and to give himself body and soul into their hands. Then pleased with their morning's work, they left their new slave in the porter's care, who gave him some coarse food, and afterwards set him to his daily tasks.

Poor Yoreth's troubles now began in earnest. By day he was employed in the hardest and most disagreeable kind of work, and at night he slept in a damp cell on a pallet of straw. He was sent out into the city to labour, and sometimes to beg, for his masters, and if in any way he failed to please them he was punished with blows or deprived of food. Many a time he was tempted to strike back or to run away, but he remembered the solemn piece of writing that he had signed. Now he saw how foolish he had been, for even should he find the treasure it would not be his, since a slave can own nothing. Still he kept up his heart somehow and drudged away, waiting for the New Year. Its eve came at last. The priests were all gathered together in their chapel, holding a service which was to last into the New Year. Yoreth stole away to the quadrangle or courtyard within the building. He knew the place well, for most of his working hours had been spent there. There was a large square stone in the centre, but on the top of that stone was an image of a man in a long flowing robe and wearing a kind of crown upon his head. This image he would have to remove before he could take away the stone, and great was his fear lest the priests should find him at work, as they had such respect for the statue that they bowed every time they passed before it. How he managed to lift that heavy statue down he never could tell; nor was it much more easy to overturn the great square stone beneath. Then in his haste, and for fear of making a noise, he dug up the earth below with his fingers. After working full an hour with these imperfect tools he struck something flat. It was metal. He got his hand beneath it and raised it up, to find a plate of bronze, which, from the holes in its corners, seemed once to have been nailed upon another surface. Yoreth carried it to the lamp which burned under the gateway and read the inscription engraved upon it in old Latin characters. It ran something like this : "The temple of the God of Fear ; this first day of the year, the priests of the most excellent God sacrificed many human victims upon his altar. May the God of Fear be favourable to his worshippers."

Stung with the new disappointment, and almost beside himself with horror at the revelation of former cruelty in the place where he had hoped to find his treasure, the treasure of a loving father, Yoreth dashed the bronze tablet to the ground. In a moment the porter was upon him, and, immediately after, the whole company of the priests. It was vain for him to struggle ; they held him down by power of numbers and with many cruel blows. Then they bound him hand and foot and sent the porter to call a guard of soldiers. The soldiers came and the slave was delivered over to them charged with the crime of sacrilege or doing dishonour to sacred things. The officer of the guard took a note of the offence and led his prisoner away. Through half the width of the city the melancholy procession passed on its way to the barrack prison outside the walls, and before it reached its destination the sun was up, and the people were stirring. Yoreth noticed, as soon as he dared lift up his head, the people who looked curiously in passing at him and his captors, but he also saw one who passed by more than once looking intensely upon his tall figure, a dark-faced man in an eastern dress, whose form he seemed to know. They came at last to the guard-house and, as he entered, Yoreth saw the man with the dark face standing close at hand. He knew now who it was—his faithful friend, Abdallah.

There was no trial that day, for it was a holiday. Yoreth spent it in his cell full of sad thoughts, with a soldier pacing back and forward past the door to let him know that he was a captive as well as a slave. When night came, there was a change of guard, and about midnight he heard the new guard stop in his walk and whisper. Then there was a chinking of money, the door of the cell opened, and Abdallah threw himself upon the neck of his master's son. "Come away quickly," he whispered, "we have no time to lose." But Yoreth replied, " I cannot go, for I have sold myself and am a slave." "You could not sell yourself," Abdallah answered, " for you are not your own to sell. No man has a right to sell God's property." So he prevailed with the poor slave and led him out into the air, a free man. After walking a short distance past the guards into the country, they found horses waiting for them, and on them Yoreth and Abdallah were soon making their way across the Apennine mountains to Ortona on the Adriatic Sea. There they found a ship ready to sail for Corinth, in which they embarked. On the way Yoreth and Abdallah told their stories to each other, and both resolved to go home. So when they came to Corinth and found another vessel bound for Syria, they gladly took ship once more and bade farewell to the shores of Europe.

I need not tell how they found their way back to Babylon. On arriving there they learned that the Armenian merchant, to whom Yoreth's house was rented, had left the country, so that their old home was theirs again. They sat together like brothers, these two, and talked of the old times. Abdallah brought forth the casket containing Elgnathir's will, which he had hidden, along with other family treasures, in a secret chamber, and he and Yoreth began to study it. On the back of the parchment, where they had never looked before, they saw two things which set them thinking. One was the picture of a circle, but so shaded as to resemble a ball or globe, and round about it, in very small letters which could only be read near the light, was written, "any point on this surface may be the centre." After long study, Yoreth said, " I have read somewhere that two great philosophers, hundreds of years ago, thought this world on which we live

was round like a ball, so that you might arrive in India by sailing far out from the pillars of Hercules between Spain and
Africa. Then is not this world the City of the Great King?
But we must wait almost another year before we search
again." "Not so," answered Abdallah, for see what is
written here from the holy book of Exodus : "This month
shall be unto you the beginning of months ; it shall be the first
month of the year to you." And then it says below : "The
true New Year comes with the new life." They looked over
the parchment very carefully now, but there was nothing
more to be seen. Then Yoreth cried, "Abdallah, the new
life is at hand ; bring the picks and spades, and let us
away."

So they went away, Yoreth and Abdallah. Surely, you say,
they had had enough of travelling and disappointment and
suffering. Yes, indeed, but this time they did not go far ;
only to the familiar court yard in the middle of his good
father's house where Yoreth as a child had often played, to
the flat stone in the centre, all written over with wonderful
characters, on which, as a young man, he had sometimes lain
at full length on bright summer nights and looked reverently
into the starry heavens. It was easy work lifting that stone,
for faith and hope made their arms strong. There was no
need for the spades, for the great treasure-chest lay all
exposed on the surface with Yoreth's name engraved upon
the lid. No key was there, but an inserted piece of metal
showed the spring that Yoreth pressed with his finger, when
open flew the chest. What a sight to behold, the silver,
the gold, the precious stones, rubies, emeralds, sapphires,
diamonds ! It was true what the will had said ; Yoreth was
the richest man in the world. At any rate there were none
richer. So all these years you think were lost. No, they had

been spent for the most part in honest search and they had taught the young Babylonian a great lesson, a lesson he was ready to give to those who looked for treasures, hidden treasures, left to them. To such he would always say, " Go and search at home." On his father's treasures, though all this happened hundreds of years ago, Yoreth is living now and will live for evermore. As for Abdallah, he still ministers to his master's children.

——

The kingdom of heaven is like unto treasure hid in a field. It is not in heaven above, nor in the earth beneath ; for, as Jesus Christ said even to wicked men when He was upon earth : " The kingdom of God has come unto you." Yet people are always seeking for it in holy places, as if all the earth were not equally holy as God's footstool, and equally unholy as sinful man's abode. One seeks the kingdom or the treasure in the glory and beauty of the world, in nature and art and literature, calling each of them the secret of life and the source of happiness. Another will find it in a pure code of morals, such as was laid down upon Mount Sinai, and confirmed on Mounts Ebal and Gerizim. To a third it lies in conformity with the powers that rule the nations, so that Mahommedanism is a great treasure for the Moslem, Brahminism for the Hindoo, and Buddhism for the Chinese. A fourth seeks his reward in slavish submission to priest-craft which fetters the soul. The kingdom of heaven, the hidden treasure, the gift of God, the testament of our Father, is Jesus Christ. Where shall we find him ? Not in any object of nature or production of art or literature, not in any creed or code, nation or church. Each and all of these may help us in our search, but He is not in any of them for us.

Just where we are, be it the very Babylon of the world, is the treasure to be found. In our own hearts and upon our own lips it lies, for if we believe with our hearts and confess with our lips Him who came to save sinners and is near to all that call upon Him, we shall have the treasure, we shall be saved. And as we must find the heavenly treasure where we are or just as we are, so we must find it not on any special day or at any special time of life. The year of God's redeemed is come. Now is the accepted time, now is the day of salvation.

The Good Lord of the Giant Mountains.

12

The Good Lord of the Giant Mountains.

"Perfect love casteth out fear."—I John, iv, 18.

Between Silesia and Bohemia there is a chain of mountains called the mountains of the Giants. Silesia is now a province of Prussia, and Bohemia, a part of the Austrian empire. But the mountains were there long ages before Austria and Prussia gave their names to German nations. And the people who lived among the Giant's mountains in the old days were not Germans but Sclaves, a rude but peaceful and kindly race of men. They dwelt in little villages upon the slopes of the smaller mountains, cultivated patches of land in the valleys, hunted the game in the forests, and caught the fish in the streams. Sometimes travelling merchants, whom we would call pedlars, paid them a visit. These were short red haired men who came all the way from the land of the Beormas near the Ural Mountains, and dark featured Greeks from the shores of the Black Sea. Sometimes, too, wandering bands of Goths or Germans found their way into the valleys, killing and plundering wherever they went, and then the peaceful Sclaves would leave their villages and flee for refuge to the thickly wooded hills. Woe to the poor Sclaves who were found on the road by these fierce invaders. Whether men, women or children it made no difference ; they were put to death as if they were wild beasts.

Now, in one of these villages among the mountains there
lived a good man and his wife, who tilled a little piece of
ground and managed to make a comfortable home for themselves by their industry.   One of the red-haired little
Beorma pedlars, whom they had kindly taken into their
house and nursed during his sickness in their village, showed
his gratitude by telling father Lubli, for that was the name
of his host, how he might increase his wealth.   He took
Lubli with him over the mountains to rocky places here and
there, where loose stones and pieces of ore were lying on
the surface to which the good Sclave had never paid any
attention.   Picking out a stone from among the others in
each place the Beorma pedlar made him notice the difference between it and the others round about.   "This one,"
he said, as he broke a reddish brown stone with another
and showed Lubli the shining yellow heart within, " is the
kind of stone we in Beormaland burn to make copper."
" And this," he went on, taking up a fragment from another
place consisting of white stone and crystals of something
like steel, "gives us two things, lead and silver."   " But
here is a stone," he continued, putting one with a silver
white face into the hand of his friend, " which, if it is treated properly, gives three different things all useful in their
way, for sulphur is found in it, and a powder that gives a
beautiful blue colour to all it touches, and another powder
which the Greeks call arsenic, a deadly poison, but good
for making yellow and green dyes and other things beside.
Remember what I have told you, and, when traders come,
keep a quantity of these stones to exchange with them for
what they have to sell."   So Lubli thanked his friend, and
at once set to work to gather the variegated copper pyrites
and galena and cobalt ores which had been pointed out to

him. When he had gathered a large quantity he gave it to the Beorma, who engaged a number of the villagers to carry it for him in the direction of his far off home. Then the pedlar went his way, promising to bring back a large share of the price he should get for the ores when he returned the following year.

Before the time arrived for the Beorma's return there came great joy to the house of Lubli. A little boy was born and lay in his mother's arms, a little boy, gentle and quiet but very timid, who hardly dared to look up in his father's happy face. But he was not sickly. He thrived well and grew every day healthy and strong, although he still started at the sound of his father's manly voice, and cowered down in his mother's arms like a little frightened hare. His mother wished him called after his father, as Lubli was a good name, but the father said " No, we must call him what he is, a timid little creature, and if he should change in after years then we can change his name. He shall be Truss just now." The mother did not like the name, for it made her think of some one who shivered or trembled with fear. But as her husband loved the truth, and she could not deny that her child was what he called it, she had to submit and introduce her son to the neighbours as " baby Truss." It was not a very real introduction, for the greeting was all on the neighbours' side. Baby Truss seemed afraid of every-body but his mother. Though he had pretty lips and bright full eyes, he would neither smile upon them with the one nor look at them with the other. Soon as a strange voice or step was heard in the house, down went the little head with the face towards the mother's breast. Then Lubli, though he loved the boy with all a father's heart, would laugh and say , " Was I not right to call this burrow-

ing little rabbit by the name of Truss, the frightened one?"
But the mother would pat the little infant gently and
answer, " For all that, he is my second Lubli and some day
he will be a brave fearless man."

All the time that Lubli could spare from his fields and his
family he gave to seeking out and gathering the stones which
the Beorma had shown him, so that by the time the pedlar
arrived he had a large quantity of each kind laid away in
caves among the mountains.   The Beorma came and made
Lubli and Lubli's wife glad with the many things he brought,
altogether too fine for their humble home.   Knives of bright
shining steel were there, and silver cups, and cloth fit for the
dress of a great lady, and, last of all, broad pieces of gold
money bearing the likeness of strange-looking eastern kings.
He said to Lubli, " This is your share of the price I obtained
for the ores I took with me.   It would have been more if it
had not cost so much to carry the heavy stones such a long.
distance.   And then I found that the rocks that gave copper
and lead and silver could be got much nearer Beormaland, so
that it is not worth while taking them all the way from the
Giant's mountains.   But the other stone which yields the
arsenic and the blue dye is not to be had in our mountains,
and as our people must have it, I will gladly take all you can
collect."   So Lubli took the pedlar over the hills and showed
him his great store of cobalt ores.   " I can never carry away
all this lot of ore," said the Beorma, " but I will tell you what
to do.   I know how the dyestuffs are taken out of the ore,
and will show you how to make a furnace with a chamber
above to catch the arsenic as it goes off in smoke, and to mix
the burnt stone that remains with powdered flints so as to
get the blue dye.   Then, instead of carrying away so much
useless stone, I will have a more precious load in a smaller

bundle. Only be careful how you work among the fumes of the arsenic, for it is a deadly poison. Soon you will become a rich man and I will not be poor." Lubli was sorry to have had the trouble of collecting his copper and lead ore for nothing, yet as he saw that the Beorma's advice was good, and as he was anxious to become rich for the sake of his wife and little Truss, he agreed to his proposal. That very week he set about building the furnace close by the place where the cobalt ore was most abundant, and, under the direction of his friend, soon had it in working order.

The Beorma travelled farther into the south and west, selling his goods and exchanging them for articles that he could sell elsewhere, while Father Lubli worked at his furnace. He had enough money now to hire men to till his little farm, so that he might give all his time to extracting the valuable cobalt and arsenic from the ores. When the good pedlar returned to the Giant's mountains on his way home, Lubli had great stores of these chemicals to give him, and already saw that he was going to become very rich. And so it came to pass, for the next visit of the Beorma brought him much gold and silver, which he hid in a safe place lest the Gothic plunderers should visit the valleys and take his wealth away. Thus the years passed by, the pedlar going with the productions of Lubli's furnace, and returning with their price in good money. Lubli built a large house, bought more land, employed many servants, and became the lord of several valleys round about his house. In the meanwhile Baby Truss grew up to be a lively active boy, fond of the free life of the hills. He had got to know his father by this time and was no longer afraid of him, but used to go with him to the cobalt mines and the smelting furnace. Lubli would not allow his son to help him in burning the ores, for he was afraid that the fumes of the arsenic would poison the boy. It was strange, when he was so careful of young Truss, that he should not have been more mindful of his own health. But he was so anxious to make money, that he forgot all about himself, and did not notice, what his wife saw only too plainly, that, although his complexion was clear and bright, his health was suffering and becoming worse year by year. So through the day Truss had the mountains to himself with the roe-bucks and the hares, and in the evening, when his father's work was done, he brought him home. These evenings were full of pleasure for the boy. His father, or his mother if Lubli were tired, told him stories of wonderful people and things that he had not seen himself, stories of distant lands and strange peoples, of fairies and dwarfs and giants, and, above all, of the two great giants whose dwelling-place was not far away, the Tchernibog and the Belibog. The Tchernibog was a black and ugly giant who lived under the ground and only came forth at night, or at least in the dark-ness, to do harm in the world. Belibog, or the white giant, was beautiful and good like the Balder of the Norsemen, and his home was a glorious palace on the highest peak of the Giant Mountains. "All this country belongs to Belibog," said the kind mother; "it was he who gave us our little farm, who sent the Beorma pedlar to our house to make us rich, and who brought you, a little helpless babe, into our arms to take care of for him. Whenever you are in trouble go and find the good giant, and never forget what he has done for us all." Young Truss promised that he would, but he trembled as he spoke and turned his eyes away, for, if he was timid before ordinary strangers, how would he dare to face this great giant of whom everybody was afraid. He remembered that once when he was with his father's servants, gathering wood in the forest to make charcoal, a great storm arose over their heads, and, as a loud peal of thunder seemed to fill all the world with its deafening noise, one of them said, " It is the voice of Belibog."

The Beorma came no more to the valleys. He, too, had grown rich and had built himself a beautiful house in Beormaland. But his servants came in his place to receive the cobalt and the arsenic and bring back the money which Lubli hid away. Alas ! poor Lubli, his wealth brought him little joy. Every day he toiled like a slave in the heat of his furnace, for he would not allow anybody to share the task of attending to it ; others might bring the ore and the charcoal, but he only must know how to make money out of them. Every year he became weaker, yet he still stuck to his work although, after a long night's coughing, he rose in the morning worse than when he went to bed. At last the cough never left him, and he who was once the strongest man in his village became thin as a ghost and feeble as a child. His brave spirit and love for his wife and son kept him up, however, longer than most of those who work at such a deadly trade as arsenic making. But, when young Truss's eighteenth birthday came, he could work no longer. That day he took to his bed, and three days later his wife was a widow and his son was fatherless. The neighbours and faithful servants came in to comfort them in their great sorrow, and found them inconsolable. Then came the funeral, when all the people of the valleys followed the rude coffin over the mountains to a shady nook near the deserted furnace where Lubli had wished to be buried. Truss was there as the chief mourner, but his mother was so stricken down with grief that she could not go with him. With a sad heart Truss laid his father's body in the grave, and then, gathering a few wild flowers from the spot, he returned in the great company of mourners.

As the funeral procession reached the top of the hill overlooking the village, from which it had set out a few hours before, there arose from the lips of all a terrible cry. The village was in flames and Lubli's great house was blazing more fiercely than the rest. Beyond the village, here and there among the fields, the scattered dwellings of the farmers were burning also, so that it was plainly no accident which had set them on fire. What could it be? All answered, " It is the Goths, the plunderers !" They had no weapons, these brave men, except their hunting knives. Their bill hooks and axes and boar spears were in their burning homes. But they cut out of the forest stout clubs and hurried down into the valley with Truss at their head, full of fierce revengeful thoughts and a wild despair. When they reached the village not a living soul was to be seen, neither friend or foe, but, about a quarter of a mile along the road, they spied a moving company, and knew that the Goths who had done the cowardly deed in their absence were there, and there, too, perhaps, were their wives and children, prisoners among these savage slave stealing enemies. A few of the villagers remained to fight the flames and save any of their friends who might be in the burning houses. The rest, with Truss as their leader, picking up a few hatchets and spears on their way, ran eagerly forward along the road in pursuit of the plunderers. Fearing lest the Goths should see them and escape, Truss led his company off the road, or path, for it was little more, farther up the mountain side, by ways that he had often travelled ; and, as his Sclaves were quick of foot, he soon brought them to a spot just above the point of the road on which the enemy was moving. Quietly descending the hill in a slanting direction, so as to keep always a little in advance of the Goths, the villagers at last came upon them, and, with wild cries and uplifted weapons, rushed into their ranks. The Goths fought bravely, for they were good soldiers and had a great contempt for the Sclaves, but the terrible rage of these poor men prevailed over their enemies' courage and better arms. Not a Goth was left alive upon the scene. All the plunder was taken back from the spoilers, and not only the plunder of their own village but that of others beside which had suffered in the same way. But, better still, in the group of terror-stricken captives whom the Goths had driven before them, many of the villagers found wives and mothers, sisters and children whom but for their bravery they would never have seen again.

Among these captives Truss looked for his mother in vain. Now he wished that he had staid behind with the old men to fight the fire and save the people in the houses. The villagers thanked and praised him, but he hardly heard them. His only thought was for his mother. More rapidly even than he had come, he sped back again to the village. He threw away axe and spear though red with the blood of many enemies, for they could not save her who was more to him than all the company he left, and they hindered his bounding steps. He reached his father's house. The faithful men who staid behind had left their own dwellings burning in their anxiety to save it. The fire was subdued and some rooms were still standing, the rooms in which his mother was most likely to be. "Is she there?" he cried as he ran forward to the door. The men answered very quietly and respectfully : "Yes, she is there," and stood aside to let him pass. He entered, and in his mother's own room, upon her bed, she lay all quietly, without an answering word to her son's cry of joy or a kiss for his warm embrace. Truss did not understand at first what the old men had taken in at a single glance. He was motherless as well as fatherless. The Goths had not harmed her, for her eyes were closed before they came, and these fierce men did not war with the dead. But the brave youth, whom all the savage band had not daunted, was stricken to the ground by the touch of a lifeless clay-cold hand. Others carried the second bier over the hill-tops to the grave beside the forge, for the son, in his great love and double sorrow, had lost his reason for a while and wandered away, none knew where, into the forest haunts of his youthful days.   Just as they were about to lower the coffin into the ground he appeared,—a wild figure, pale and haggard, and threw himself upon it ; and, his strength fairly exhausted with hunger and unrest, fainted there. Kindly hands removed him, strong arms carried him back to his now desolate home, and gentle women nursed him through his long fever into returning health.

When Truss came to himself again he was poor.   True, he had the ruins of his father's house and much land, but he had nothing to keep the house with or to pay labourers for tilling his fields.   His mother had known where Lubli's wealth was hidden for he had told her, but she had had no opportunity of telling her son.   He searched everywhere as soon as he was strong enough to go about, among the ruins of the house, in the furnace-room over the hills, in every cave and mining shaft, but found nothing.   His father had never taught him his trade lest it should injure his health, so that he had nothing to exchange with the Beorma pedlars.   One night, full of sad thought, he lay down upon his couch, having toiled all day at one little field. The other fields were going to ruin, for the villagers were not rich enough to buy them, and had enough to do to cultivate their own. Truss lay wondering where his daily bread was to come from, and wondering, too, why such dreadful trials should have fallen upon him more than on others. In the morning he did not recollect any dream of the night, but his mother's words kept ringing in his ears, "Whenever you are in trouble, go and find the good giant." Now Truss was Truss still, that is he was timid and retiring in his nature, and doubtful of new friends. True, he had been very brave in his conflict with the Goths, but that was because his love for his mother was so great that it overcame his fears. He had never seen Belibog. He had only his father's and mother's word for it that there was such a giant, and that he would receive him kindly. Sometimes indeed he had seen from a distance the high mountain on the top of which his castle was built, but it was so far away and the clouds were so thick about its summit that Truss had never seen the castle. Still he was in great and sore trouble, so he determined in spite of his fears to take his dead mother's advice.

Away then on the longest journey he had ever taken went Truss. He had no money in his wallet to pay his way, nor any food to take its place. He would not borrow, although there were people willing to lend him money, for he wished the good giant to know how poor he was. Still he wanted for nothing. The weather was fine and it was no hardship to sleep in the open air under the stars of heaven. There were nuts and wild fruits in the valleys, and fish and game to be caught or knocked down in the streams and forests. He had flint and steel to give him fire when he wanted it.

Several days passed in this way, and then he arrived at the foot of Belibog's mountain. The mountain itself was high and vast, and like the mountain was everything upon it. Such great frowning cliffs of rock Truss had never seen, nor such gigantic trees. The large birds and animals terrified him, although the beasts did not seek to do him harm, and the birds sang very sweetly. The very grass was high above his head, and the wild flowers so wide that he could only see one petal at a time. He could have built a house on a single blossom. The straight road up the mountain was so broad that all the people of his native village could have walked abreast upon its gentle incline. Up this road with fear and trembling went Truss and stood at last before the castle of the mighty giant. The gates were wide open, so that he did not need to knock, but he was so afraid of presuming on Belibog's goodness that he tapped feebly upon the lower edge of one of them that he could just reach with his hand. Then he heard a great footstep which seemed to shake the mountain and the castle upon it and made him quake with terror. In a moment the giant stood before him and said in so gentle a voice that Truss could hardly believe it came from him, " Welcome Truss, son of Lubli ; what do you wish me to do for you?" Truss was astonished to find that Belibog knew his name and that of his father, but it gave him back some courage, so he told his story very shortly and begged the giant to help him. Belibog looked at Truss in a very kindly way, for he was pleased with the young man's confidence. Truss, however, did not notice this, for the giant towered so high above him that his eyes never reached farther than the buckles on his shoes. Then Belibog told him that his father's treasure had been buried in the earth near a great cave in the lead mine, and that Tchernibog, who dwelt in that cave, had taken it under his care. " But," he said, " go to the place alone and take the treasure, and if Tchernibog or his servants come to hinder you, tell them that Belibog has commanded you to do it. They will leave you alone. Then trade with that money in many lands. When you are in trouble call upon me. When you are happy do not forget me. Some day when you know me better you shall bring all your wealth into this castle, where it will be safe always, and you shall live with me as my son." Truss thanked the kind giant and promised never to forget him. Just then he would like to have staid with his great protector, but as he went down the mountain and saw all the beautiful world coming in sight he felt that it was good to live in that world. And yet a little while before it had seemed to him a place only of sorrow and suffering. That night and the next and all that passed till he returned to his village, Truss thought of the giant, and repeated his name over and over so that anyone who wished to do him harm might be afraid at the sound of it and leave him alone.

Truss reached his home in the daylight, and the same evening when the sun had set and the clear bright moon shone high in the heavens, went forth to the lead mine to find his father's treasure. He had no trouble in finding the place; indeed there was a stone there to mark it, and on that stone the words were written " Lubli's gift to his son Truss." Now the young man longed to thank the good father who had given his life to make him rich. He remembered Belibog and thanked him in his heart instead. Then he opened up the earth and began to remove the treasure. What a disturbance there was then ! Out of the cave near by came troops of ugly black dwarfs, and at their back the black giant Tchernibog himself. The dwarfs clustered round about Truss like vicious wasps, grinning hideously, screaming with horrid cries, pulling at his clothes and bidding him leave the treasure. The loud voice of Tchernibog told him to let it rest where it was, then said there was no treasure there, and afterwards offered him a better treasure if he would come into his cave. Truss was much afraid, but when he heard the black giant tell such contradictory falsehoods he saw how foolish it would be to pay any attention to what he said. So he drew himself up very proudly, though he trembled all the while, and said with a loud voice " Belibog wishes it." Then the dwarfs scuttled back into the cave in a great fright, and Tchernibog left him with a scowl of baffled rage on his black face. With a bright and happy heart Truss shouldered the treas-ure, heavy though it was, and made his way home without any further trouble. That morning, as he rested after his toil, he dreamt that his father and mother came to his bed-side and blessed him, while Belibog looked down upon them all with a very kindly smile.

Now Truss became a merchant. He left his native valleys where the people were poor, and visited richer lands. Perhaps if he had known how to make cobalt and arsenic he would have staid there all his life. He visited the rich towns on the Mediterranean and on the Black Sea ; went to the country of the Beormas, and to Persia and other East-ern lands of which the Beormas told him. He even crossed the Mediterranean into Africa in search of new articles of commerce. Truss became very rich, so rich that he forgot all about his old home among the Giant Mountains, and his great benefactor the giant Belibog. He was at home everywhere, for in all places he had business and the merchant princes of the world esteemed him highly. He thought his happiness was going to last forever. But he was mistaken. In the wild country between the land of the Beormas and the Black Sea, where the Don Cossacks now dwell, he was taken suddenly ill. There were no physicians there, not even a nurse to watch by him, none but his servants who sold his goods and drove the beasts that made up his caravan. The only thought of these servants was that if he should die they would be able to share his property. So they left him as much alone as they could. Truss saw death staring him in the face and all his treasures thus melting away out of his hands. There was no one to help him. Yes, there was one whom he had forgotten, who had given him these treasures when he was very poor. He cried in agony, " Belibog, Belibog, come and save me." Belibog came and laid his hand upon the sick man, and that hand was all Truss saw, so gentle, so refreshing, so full of new strong life that the dying merchant revived, but so great that as he looked at it he wished it away, for he feared that with the slightest clasp or incautious movement it might crush him out of existence. Yet when he arose from his bed and entered on his travels and business again, he could not forbear telling his ungrateful servants that Belibog had come to his help. Perhaps he did so more to make them afraid than to express his gratitude.

Again all went well with him for a time. A physician travelled constantly in his train for fear of sickness in lonely regions. But there are other troubles as well as sickness in the world. Truss had opened a trade with the seaport towns of northern Africa, and, as he saw that it would be a very profitable one, he embarked all that he possessed in a

ship sailing from Italy, and himself accompanied his possessions.   A great storm arose in the midst of the sea.   The
terrified sailors gave up in despair all attempts to manage
the vessel, which tossed about like a toy upon the huge
waves.   Truss knew nothing about managing a ship and
his physician was just as wise.   Already many bales of
merchandise that had been stored on deck for want of room
below had been washed overboard, and the trader saw
no hope of saving the rest.   Yes, there was hope.   He
stood upon the deck holding on by the bulwarks, with his
face towards the land of his birth, and called over the
stormy waters, " Belibog, Belibog, do not suffer me to perish."   Then a white shining arm shot out towards the
vessel and set it upon an even keel.   A voice too that he
knew well said majestically, " Be still."   It was for two
that the voice came, for the storm on the sea and the tempest of dread in the merchant's heart.   In a moment both
were at rest, but was it not strange that Truss shrank from
the powerful arm and trembled with a new kind of terror at
the welcome voice ?   Again as the arm withdrew and the
voice was heard no more Truss gave thanks with a feeling
of relief.   The ship went safely on her way, discharged her
cargoes in the African ports, and doubled the wealth of her
owner.

Truss was not satisfied yet with his riches.   He heard that
on the other side of the great sandy desert, which lies to the
south of the fertile strip that bounds the Mediterranean Sea,
there were savage peoples, rich in gold and ivory, who would
pay him large prices for his goods.   Accordingly he prepared a great caravan of camels, loaded them with merchandise and all things necessary for the journey, and set off
under the direction of good guides for the land of gold and

ivory. The caravan crossed the desert safely and arrived in
the country of the barbarians. These were only too glad to
exchange gold and pearls, ivory and precious stones for the
articles the merchant had brought with him, and to pay him
such prices as he had never got before. Then, when he was
anxious to return, they entreated him to wait a little while, as
the season of the winds was coming on, during which it was
not safe to cross the waste of shifting sand. Truss was not
willing to delay, for he wanted to turn the things he had got
from the savage people into money or other goods in some
favourable market. Back therefore came the caravan upon
its old track. For a few days all went well. Then the
wind began to blow and the fine sand was carried by it in
great clouds right in the face of the company. The guides
lost their way. Days passed and nights, in which the caravan had to keep moving for fear of being buried in the
rapidly forming sandbanks, and still there was no sight of
the green shores of the dreary ocean of dust. The store of
water which the camels carried in their stomachs was
exhausted after five days, and as there was none to spare for
them they died of thirst, with the exception of the best which
were allowed a share from the waterbags. The drivers and
even the guides became exhausted, lay down to sleep and
were soon buried under the sand. Again Truss saw death
near at hand and his riches about to vanish. Twice he had
been saved by his great protector. He thought of these deli.
verances, and once more with all his strength prayed Belibog
to come and rescue him. When he prayed the fierce African
sun was shining down upon his head and the hot sand burned
his feet. The wind, full of dust, was close and stifling. In
a moment all was changed. A great rock, cool and refreshing, that kept off the fiery breath of the storm and moistened

the very sands beneath him, suddenly rose before his face. And yet it was no rock, for it lived and moved. It was a great body that held a living soul, full of kindness for the parched and weary traveller. It was indeed Belibog, though Truss did not see his face nor hear a word from his lips. The camels that remained came into the shelter, and the drivers, though they knew not what it was. There, for a time, they were refreshed, and, after pleasant sleep, rose to pursue their journey. The great rock was gone, but the fierce scorching wind had ceased, the hot sun had set, and after a short night's journey, the welcome sight of palm trees and grass appeared. Again Truss gave thanks to Belibog, but half shuddered as he thought of that gigantic form. " If it had fallen upon me," he thought, "I should have been crushed into nothingness." It was this fear of his that made the loving giant depart from him as soon as he gave relief.

Truss was very rich now and did not care to risk his wealth any more by sea or land. He thought often of Belibog and all the good he had done to him. He thought also of his father and mother, asleep among his native mountains. He determined to go there, where he would be near his giant friend and the memories of those who had loved him. So he crossed the sea with his possessions and landed on the Dalmatian coast. There he engaged many servants with horses and mules to carry his baggage and his stores of gold and silver and jewels overland to the Giant Mountains. All went well with him and his party until they arrived on the borders of his native land. There he found his way blocked by an army of Goths, who held possession of the only pass through the valley by which horses might go. Looking behind him he saw also that another body of enemies was coming up rapidly in that direction to hinder his retreat.

His servants saw all that he beheld and were panic-stricken. He called on them to fight, but they threw down their arms and ran to the hills for safety, leaving their master alone with the animals and their costly burdens. In his distress Truss lifted his eyes to the great Giant Mount where Belibog dwelt ; and that look, so watchful was the giant, brought him to the side of his ungrateful friend. On came the host on either side, and with them came a great company swarming out of the earth led by the black Tchernibog, who longed to be revenged on Belibog and Truss. The merchant trembled now with a terrible fear, for all the world seemed to be on one side and only his giant protector on the other. But Belibog placed himself in front of Truss, telling him to remain quiet and trust him. The Gothic hordes and the swarms of Tchernibog had united now and filled the valley, standing in dense masses opposite their great enemy. He did not move. There was no weapon in his hand. They called to him to surrender, but he did not heed their wild cries. Then their arrows darkened the air, and many pierced him. They came nearer and threw their javelins ; then rushed upon him with their spears. Then the giant fell straight forward. They saw him tottering, and, fearing, sought to flee, but there was no room to escape. Down, crushing all along the valley, came the gigantic form upon the heads of his enemies. Their weapons had pierced him, but his fall was their destruction. As he fell he turned and lay there with his face upward to the sky.

Truss came forth and saw his enemies slain. But his friend, his only friend, was slain too, and all for him. He could not understand such love, he could hardly believe it. He went up to the dead giant without any fear but with a sad heart, as he thought of his suspicions and ingratitude in the past, and with such sorrow of love as even his mother's death had not filled him. He was not afraid of those hands all pierced with darts and arrows, nor of that great noble form, that had sheltered him in the desert, in which was the point of many a spear. He gazed for the first time upon the face of Belibog, calm, radiant and beautiful in death, and wearing a look of infinite tenderness. He lay down beside his friend, forgetting his wealth, forgetting all the world, and wept as if his heart would break. Then he crept inside the outstretched arm and pillowed his head upon the giant's breast, and thought amid his sobs of the wonderful love he had learned so late to know. What time passed by, Truss could not tell, for he had lost all thought of time, all thought of everything but this body on which his head was pillowed. But all at once there was a movement like an earthquake. He himself was lifted up. Brushing away his tears, he saw himself in the giant's arms, and Belibog, his friend, the white, the strong, the beautiful, was bending over him the face of wondrous kindness, and saying " Lovest thou me ?" What could Truss say but " Lord, thou knowest that I love thee." What could he do but cling closer to the arm that was about him. " Then," answered Belibog, " thy name shall no longer be Truss, the fearful, but Lubli, the loving. Come, let us go home." So the giant that had been dead arose, because he was a giant and not a man, and with Lubli, who had once been Truss, in his arms, strode up the Giant Mountain and entered the glorious palace-castle on its summit. There, too, came all Lubli's wealth that was worth removing. He found a father and a mother there, but never yet has he met with one whom he fears so little or loves so much as the giant who gave his life to save him.

If you read over the 107th psalm you will find that it contains a story something like that I have told you. Every now and again in the psalm it is written, "Then they cried unto the Lord in their trouble and he delivered them out of their distresses." And at the close we read, "Whoso is wise and will observe these things, even they shall understand the loving kindness of the Lord." We have met together to-day to worship God, because we all believe in Him and know Him to be the giver of every good and perfect gift. But many here are half afraid of this good God, and none of us trust Him as we ought. Fear is part of the heritage that sin has brought us. We see God in the great mountain of His power and holiness, and the very majesty which sits enthroned there makes us tremble. We forget that God came into the world to take away sin, and therefore to take away the fear that accompanies it. How often He has fulfilled His promise to hear us when we call upon Him. How often has He come to our help even when our cry came after a long time of forgetfulness and ingratitude. What foolish and wicked relief we have sometimes felt in losing sight of God for a time, even though he had just done us some great good. Now to cure all this let us go with Truss to the narrow valley that leads to the land of our rest. Here we see all our enemies blocking the way. They are sins, more in number than the hairs of our head. You can't kill a sin any more than you can stop the motion of an ocean wave, and bid it be as if it had never been. God can, but, so far as we know, only in one way. That is, by His own death, as God manifest in the flesh, in the person of His Son Jesus Christ. By His death He made an end of sin. Christ's death then has slain all your foes and left the way open to

peace and rest.   Your sins lie there dead beneath the crucified.   Can you doubt that love?   Can you fear Him who
lies there upon the bitter cross, nailing your offences and
your enemies to it with the wounds that rent His body and
filled His soul with agony?   And yet this is the King of
Heaven, the Lord of glory, the Creator of the ends of the
earth, the Sovereign Judge of quick and dead.   May His
perfect love perfect yours, and cast out the fear that hath
torment.   He that feareth is not made perfect in love.
God hath not given us the spirit of bondage again to fear,
but the spirit of adoption whereby we cry Abba Father.

The Prince who gave up a Throne.

●

X.

The Prince who gave up a Throne.

"All flesh is grass, and all the goodliness thereof is as the flower of the field. The grass withereth, the flower fadeth : but the word of our God shall stand forever."—ISAIAH XL. 6, 8.

Under the snow-capped Himalayas, on the borders of Kumaon and Nepaul, stood, in ancient days, the wonderful city Kapila. Its ruler, and the king of all the great Sakya land round about it, was Sudhodana of the royal race of the Sun. His land was one of the most beautiful, fertile, and rich, in all India. From its wide fields, watered by numerous streams that flowed from the mountain sides to meet the many branches of the Ganges, two harvests were reaped each year. In the orchards and along the road sides, almost all the fruit trees of India, with those of Persia in the west and Tartary in the north, grew freely. The meadows and open woods were so bedecked with fair blossoms of every kind that they might easily have been mistaken for flower-gardens. In the mountains were many mines, rich in gold and silver, in iron and lead and copper, in orpiment and borax. The forests were full of musk-deer and other game. Silk-worms swarmed over the wild mulberry trees and spun their cocoons without the help of man, and, near by them, wherever they could find a convenient hollow to build their cells, myriads of bees stored the honey they sipped from a thousand flowers. Sudhodana, therefore, was a very wealthy king, and all his subjects had enough for their daily wants. His land was beautiful enough without any improvement. Nevertheless he enclosed his palace within wide domains of park and garden, by lofty walls ; and into these domains he brought all that was most pleasing in sight and smell and taste among the flowering plants and trees of the neighbouring countries. The palaces themselves were spacious buildings, true in proportion and graceful in structure, and were adorned within with more than eastern magnificence. Large bodies of brave Sakya soldiers, each of whom was dressed and armed better than were some of the kings of India at that time, kept watch and ward over the royal palaces and grounds by night and by day. They had nothing else to do, for all the nations were at peace with the kingdom of Kapila.

The greatest of Sudhodana's treasures was his only son, Sidhartta, for his wife, Mahamaya, had died just six days after the boy was born. On this only child the father lavished all his affection, and everything he did for improving and beautifying the land was done for Sidhartta's sake. The boy grew up in the midst of luxury and all that could make him happy, as far as this world can· make happy, to be a strong, handsome, wise and good man. Yet he was never allowed to travel through the kingdom, nor to stray beyond the walls that bounded the palace grounds. The king had a reason for not permitting him to do so, and this was the reason. When the son of Mahamaya was only five days old, Sudhodana had called together the wise men of his kingdom and asked them to read the child's fortune, so that he might give him a name suitable to his destiny. After thinking for a long time, the wise men told the king that his son would not be a great monarch, for he would give up

his royalty to seek the heavenly life as a poor man, and
in doing so he would establish a new religion better than
the old worship of the heathen gods. So they recommended
that he should be called Sidhartta, the establisher. Sudhodana liked the name they had chosen and commanded that
his son should be so called, but he did not believe that Sidhartta would ever resign the great empire of the Sakyas and
become a poor man. However, when the boy arrived at
the age of twelve, the king, wondering that he was so unlike
other boys and wishing to know the reason, called the wise
men together again. When he asked them what his son
was going to become, they answered as before, although
some of the wise men whom he had first asked were dead
and their places had been taken by others. Sudhodana was
angry when he heard their answer. He said, "I do not
wish my brave, handsome boy to become a poor man and
to seek for a kingdom in the clouds, when I have the finest
kingdom in the world to give him. Besides I am a lonely
man since his mother died, and surely my boy will not leave
his father who has given him all his love." The wise men
replied, "O king, we cannot change that which is to be.
We grieve for you, but, as it will be for your son's good and
for the good of thousands more, we would not change it if
we could." Then said Sudhodana, "How will it all come
to pass? For what cause will the prince leave the kingdom
and his father." The wise men answered, "He will see the
four signs that point to a better world; old age, disease,
death, and the emptiness of earthly things. He will meet
with a happy man that owns nothing, and will follow him."
The king took a note of these five things, and, although he
said nothing more to the wise men, he determined to keep
them all far away from the sight of his beloved Sidhartta.

After the conversation with the wise men, Sudhodana had three palaces built specially for his son in the royal grounds of Kapila, suited to the three seasons of the year in that part of India We are told in the old books that the smallest was five stories high, the next, seven, and the largest, nine. The grounds were greatly enlarged and beautified around these three palaces, and guards kept constant watch, so that none of the objects which the wise men had named might be seen by the young prince. Nobody that was decrepid with age, no sick person, nothing that was in the least offensive was allowed to come within many miles of the city of Kapila. The bodies of those who died were taken away secretly by night and buried at a great distance; and all poor people were forbidden under pain of imprisonment or death, to appear near the royal gardens. Everything that could please the heir to the throne and bind his heart to his future kingdom was provided for him by his fond father. To Sudhodana's great delight Sidhartta was grateful for all this kindness, and spent his days in the full enjoyment of all sorts of worldly happiness. He now thought that the prophecies of the wise men were false. Nevertheless he ordered the guards to form a great circle of outposts at a distance of four miles all round the walls of Kapila, and gave them strict charge to stop all obnoxious persons who might seek to come into the presence of his son and give him a distaste for the things of the world. The guards loved the prince and did their duty well, turning back many of the poor and sick and infirm who might have been helped and should have been helped by the king and his heir.

One beautiful morning when the sun was softly shining, Sidhartta, wishing for a change from the life of the palace,

called the nobleman Channa who was his charioteer and
bade him bring the horses, that he might drive in the royal
park.   The horses came to the palace gate, four in number
and snowy white, all harnessed abreast to the royal chariot, in
which Sidhartta took his seat while Channa drove.   Along
the broad level roads, past garden and greensward, thicket
and orchard, smoothly went the chariot.   A gentle breeze
from the mountains fanned the air and wafted abroad the
fragrance of the flowers which the early dew had distilled.
The birds were piping their happy morning songs.   The
insects hummed cheerfully as they flitted past on golden
wing, and all the world seemed full of youth and active life·
The horses caught the infection of the morning air and
snapped playfully at each other, shaking their manes and
tossing their heads as if the drive were a mere pleasure trip
of their own.   Sidhartta and his charioteer Channa conversed gayly together as they drove onwards, feeling life to
be a blessed thing and forgetting, if indeed Sidhartta
knew, that the world brings anything else than life and
happiness.   Suddenly, however, as the chariot turned a
curve, the young prince started in his seat and clutched
Channa's arm.   Close beside them on the road was an aged
man, tottering forward with trembling steps by the aid of a
staff.   His body was bent almost half over with age and
toil, but as his head was lifted to view the royal chariot the
prince saw his long gray hair, his sunken eyes, his wrinkled
brow and toothless gums.   " What is that, Channa ?"
Sidhartta inquired.   " It is an old man, my lord," replied
the charioteer.   " Was he born like that ?" continued the
prince.   " No, your highness," Channa answered ; " he was
once young as I am ; he was born a little child."   " Are
there many such creatures in the world," said Sidhartta

again. " Alas !" replied his companion, "there are very
many." "And I," at last asked the prince, "shall I become old and feeble in time ?" Channa hesitated, but seeing his master becoming impatient, he made answer, " If
you live, my lord, which may the Gods grant, you will be
old and feeble, though not like this poor man." What does
he mean, thought Sidhartta, by if I live, and poor ? What
can I do but live ? What is it to be poor ? But he asked
no more questions of the charioteer. He looked once more
at the retreating figure of the old man, then shuddered and
said, " Let us go home." So back to the palace they drove,
and though all nature was the same as when they had come
out, somehow to them it seemed changed and shorn of half
its beauty and gladness.

Sudhodana came to meet his son on his return and asked
him if he had enjoyed his drive. Sidhartta answered that
he would never drive again, for he had seen that, as the
green leaves wither on the tree, so the youth and vigor of
manhood must fade away upon earth. " I must leave
Kapila," said the prince, " and seek for a land where there
is no old age." The King was alarmed. He questioned
the officers of the guard, and they solemnly swore that no
old man had passed through their lines. The police
searched the whole city, but .could find no old man. Then
Sudhodana told his son that what he had seen must have been
an evil vision sent by some enemy to do him harm. Sidhartta believed his father and again took part in all the
pleasures of the court, forgetting for a time what Channa
had told him. It was four months before he thought of
going out again, and in the meanwhile the King had placed
the guards at a distance of eight miles from the city and had
given them the strictest orders. Once more the white horses

carried the chariot swiftly forward over the level winding paths, and Sidhartta rejoiced in the rapid motion through the balmy air. He felt strong and vigorous, for all thought of old age had been banished from his mind since last he drove that way. Far in advance of the chariot rode the noblemen of the court, eagerly looking on every side lest any offensive person or thing should have found a way into the grounds. But, in spite of their precautions, the prince started as before when the chariot turned aside from the main road into a shady avenue that broke the force of the sun's rays. By the side of the avenue, under a spreading fig tree, lay a leper full of sores. His body was livid and wasted, and he groaned aloud in his misery. "What is that," asked Sidhartta. "A sick man, a leper, your highness," Channa replied. So the prince questioned him about sickness and disease, to learn that there was much of it in the world, that it brought pain and suffering and made life a burden, that nobody was sure of being free from it, and that it had often attacked the greatest kings. "Let us go home," cried the prince, and spoke not a word more till he reached the palace.

Sidhartta sought his father's presence and told him that he was going to leave Kapila because there was sickness and dire disease in the kingdom which nobody could cure, for he himself had seen a leper, a miserable being, yet a man like himself, whose whole body was full of sores. The King said, "You have been deceived again, my son. Come and hear what your attendants and the officers of the guard and police have to say to your story." The noblemen, who had ridden before the chariot, all answered that they had seen no leper. The captains of the guard said it was impossible that any such person could have come in without

14

their seeing him. The police, who had searched every-where in the palace grounds, in the city, and far beyond its walls, reported that there was no sick person of any kind to be found. Then Sudhodana quieted his son's fears, and ordered the guards to be posted twelve miles from the city and their numbers to be increased so as to make a complete circuit. Again Sidhartta occupied himself with the pleasures of the court.

Four months more were passed in the happy life within the palace walls, and again a fancy seized the prince to re-visit the beautiful grounds. Again the officers of the court rode far in advance of the chariot, and were delighted to find that everything was in the best of order and that there was no sign of any intruder. Channa, too, as he drove the white horses, sought to engage his master in such conversation as would lead his thoughts away from the scenes they had both witnessed on the two former occasions. Nature was as beautiful as ever in its season, and so well kept were the grounds that not even a withered leaf appeared to sug-gest the thought of decay. But Channa trembled slightly as he saw a hawk hovering in the air near at hand and then suddenly descend, quick as a flash of light, to pounce upon a little bird which was pouring out its heart in song. Happily Sidhartta's head was turned the other way, so that he did not see the little bloodstained body palpitating under the strong beak and cruel talons of the bird of prey. On went the chariot, and, avoiding the old paths in which the aged man and the leper had been met with, entered one that gave promise of pleasanter shade and wider view. All at once the horses come to a standstill. Channa urges them, but they rear and refuse to advance. He leaps from the chariot and goes forward to their heads that he may lead them past the object they fear. He sees it all too plainly. What can the officers have been about? It is a body, a dead body; already corruption has set in, and the loath-some worms are feasting there. Channa stands in despair, rooted to the spot. Then Sidhartta descends and stands beside him. "What is that dreadful thing?" he asks in a hoarse whisper which is full of horror. "It is a dead man," the charioteer replies as if he were signing his own death-warrant. So they turn the horses' heads towards the palace, and, as they drive forward, the prince questions Channa about death. He learns that his ancestors are dead and his mother; that his father, king though he is, must die; and that he, the young and vigorous Sidhartta, must some day be like that helpless, corrupting body which lies across the road. Home they go, sad at heart and with downcast eyes, as if they had been at a funeral of some near friend rather than as returning from a holiday drive.

Sidhartta retires to his own apartments and speaks to no one, not even his father. His thoughts are all of old age, disease and death. All the glory and beauty have gone out of life. It has no attractions for him. He wishes to leave a world so full of evil and seek for one in which these things will be unknown. But Sudhodana learns from the charioteer what the prince has seen and fears greatly be-cause the prediction of the wise men is being realized. The noblemen are degraded who went forward to clear the way, because of their negligence; the captains of the guard are dismissed and their places given to other soldiers, because they allowed so hideous an object to be brought into the royal park. Nevertheless, although the police and the king's servants search far and wide, they cannot find any dead body, not even a sign that such a thing has been with-

in the grounds.   In vain Sudhohana strives to cheer the
heart of his son with costly presents.   The prince's chosen
companions seek as unsuccessfully to gain admittance to his
apartments,   that they may revive his spirits and lead him
back to the world.   Channa alone is allowed to visit him,
and, when he does so, all the talk between him and his master is of what they saw during their three drives.   The mind
of Sidhartta is fully made up to renounce his father's kingdom and use all efforts to find one in which there shall be
neither old age nor disease nor death.   Still he feels that he
loves pleasant things ; to enjoy the comforts of a royal
palace ; to be surrounded with attractive objects and sweet
perfumes and melodious sounds ; to have companionship
that suits his high rank and cultivated taste.   There are many
things in the kingdom of Kapila that he would gladly keep
and enjoy, if only the three evils could be forever banished.
Yet he can see no way, nor can Channa, of removing these
three evils. All his father's wealth and power, his army and
police have not been able to keep the sight of them from
his eyes, and now that he has seen them there is nothing
that can blot them out of his memory or hinder the grief
that memory brings from gnawing at his heart.

Sudhodana did not despair.   He resolved to try again to
rouse the prince from his gloom.   In a short time his son's
birthday was to come round, and for this birthday the fond
father made great preparations.   From all parts of his kingdom he brought singers and players on instruments of
music, dancing men and women, cunning jugglers who, by
their wonderful sleight-of-hand could deceive the most prac-
tised eye, actors dressed in gorgeous raiment who were
able to imitate the real life of great kings and conquerers,
and supple-jointed tumblers, skilled to walk almost in mid-

air and throw their bodies into any shapes they pleased. A
great pavilion was set up in the fairest part of the palace
grounds capable of holding a thousand people, and in the
midst of it was placed a royal table in front of the king's
most splendid throne. A thousand lamps lit up the pavilion, and their light, falling upon the gold and crimson
hangings, filled it with a mellow, rosy radiance. Here and
there altars of incense spread abroad their sweet perfumes,
while many fountains, scattering their spray high in the air,
dispensed around a delicious coolness. Night blooming
flowers of varied hues and trees bearing yellow and scarlet
fruits shone through the rich dark green foliage, and broke
up the great expanse into a multitude of charming views,
giving relief to the eye wherever it rested. In many circles,
gradually widening round the pavilion, the Sakya soldiers
stood on guard, to hinder any intruder from marring the
scene of perfect delight which the loving father had prepared
in honour of his son.

The birthday came. Sudhodana sought his son's apartments, and was admitted because of the occasion. Tenderly
he embraced Sidhartta and begged him for this once to
please his father, and show himself to the courtiers who
loved him and to the people he had brought from all parts
to perform in his honour. Channa added his entreaties to
those of Sudhodana, and at length Sidhartta was overcome
and promised to grace the festival with his presence. The
day soon passed by, and when night came Sidhartta looked ·
forth from his balcony and saw the pavilion down below
glowing like a great half moon that rested its face upon the
earth. He clothed himself in his costliest dress and adorned
it with his richest jewels. Then, attended by Channa and
many officers of his household, he went forth through the

lines of soldiers, who bowed the knee and presented arms
as he passed to the pavilion.   The prince had been brought
up in luxury all his life and had seen many beautiful and
wonderful sights, but never before had his father provided
for him such a joyful surprise.   Dazzled with the light and
the splendour, his ears charmed with the music of voices
and instruments in perfect tune, and almost intoxicated
with the odours of incense and flowers, he advanced
towards the royal table and the throne.   On the throne
Sudhodana was sitting, but, when he beheld his beloved
son, he came forward and, embracing him before the assembled company, led Sidhartta to the seat of majesty;
then took his own place on a more humble couch beside
him.   Thereupon all the nobles cried, " Long life our prince
Sidhartta," and the trumpets blared and the drums beat,
while all in the pavilion stood up and shouted.   Outside, the cry was caught up by the Sakya soldiers, circle
after circle, till it died in the far off distance miles away ;
and the drums of each division rolled like ceaseless thunder,
and the spears and swords clashed upon the brass and iron
of the warriors' shields like the clang of unnumbered hosts
in deadly conflict.   Sidhartta forgot his vows, his visions,
his thoughts.   He only felt that to be king of Kapila was
to be lord of the earth.   All that night the prince seemed
to be in a happy dream.   Attendants covered the tables
with royal dainties and wines cooled with Himalayan
snows.   The courtiers, following their master's example,
ate and drank and were merry.   The singing men and
women sang their sweetest songs ; the players on instruments played softly ; the actors pleased the eye with their
gorgeous representations of ancient days ; and loud shouts
of laughter and rounds of applause greeted the tricks of the

conjurors, the nimble feats of the tumblers and the graceful movements of the dancers. Sudhodana was gratified beyond all measure with his son's enjoyment of the scene, but, as his preparations for it had 'wearied him, he took his leave when half the night was spent and retired to rest, a happy man.

Before morning came, Sidhartta fell asleep upon his throne. Then, as nobody dared leave the pavilion while the prince remained, and as nobody dared to rouse him from his slumbers, others soon followed his example. At once the music was hushed and the performances ceased. As there were none to watch them and they had nothing to do, the singers and actors, and even the attendants, sat down to the tables, helping each other to the remnants of the feast which they ate and drank without stint. The lamps and incense altars were neglected, and what an hour before had been a scene of perfect order and beauty, was now one of confusion and riot. The morning came and the beams of the Indian sun shone upon the pavilion. One bright warm ray fell upon Sidhartta and he awoke. What a spectacle met his eye. The wicks of the lamps had burned down in their sockets and gave forth an unpleasant smell of burning oil and cotton. The incense was all gone from the altars, and the coals that remained upon them filled the air with deadly charcoal fumes. The ground was littered with remnants of the feast, and even the marble basins of the fountains were full of the rinds and husks of fruit. On every side lay sleeping men and women, some with their heads upon the tables, others lying upon the couches, and others stretched full length upon the floor, with their instruments and conjuring toys, their acting masks and serving vessels in confusion round about them.

Their clothes were in disorder, their hair dishevelled, their
bodies in ungraceful postures. Some were sleeping the
heavy sleep of the drunkard ; some tossed feverishly from
side to side, gnashing their teeth and speaking meaningless
words ; while others, waking like himself, yawned listlessly
as if they were coming out of a great weariness. Even
Channa's arms were folded on the table before him, and
his head was pillowed upon them. Sidhartta rose with a
soul full of disgust, for he had seen the vanity of all earthly
things, even of the fairest that the eye of man ever beheld.
Forth from the pavilion he went over the prostrate bodies
of the revellers into the morning light. The soldiers were
on guard still, but the night air had chilled their enthusi-
asm, and their long watch had wearied them. They bowed
the knee and presented arms as he passed, but no cheer
left their lips like that which the night before had filled the
prince's heart with pride. Beauty and glory are fleeting
visions, he said to his sad soul, as he went his solitary way
to the palace, there to take a troubled sleep upon his silken
couch. And as he slept, the dream, which came again and
again before his spirit eyes, was one of a land where joys
are never ending.

When Sidhartta awoke finally out of his broken sleep,
the day was declining. The courtiers had not dared to
come near him, so ashamed were they of their conduct the
night before. Channa alone came and entreated forgiveness for the crime of sleeping in his master's presence.
The prince willingly pardoned his faithful servant, and
then they went out together to walk in the grounds nearest
the city. Every one they met on their way was excited
about something or other. Some were grieving over the
past, others were doubtful of the future, while others again

were eagerly pressing forward to the possession of a new object of happiness. Sidhartta said to Channa, " Is there no happy man, no quiet satisfied soul in all this world, no heart of perfect peace?" The charioteer answered, " My Lord, we shall see," for as the prince spoke, he beheld before him the figure of a recluse who had given up the pleasures of the world to do good. Soon they stood before this man whose dress was poor and mean, his form slight and emaciated, but his eyes, which looked but a short distance before him, were full of quiet light and his whole face betokened rest and peace. " Who are you?" asked Sidhartta, " and why are you so composed and calm in the midst of a busy, unsatisfied, pleasure-seeking world?" The recluse replied, " My Lord, I am a man who believes in a better world than this, and all my thoughts I give so to spend this present life and overcome the love of this present world that I may be judged worthy of entering on the happy state hereafter." Thereupon he courteously saluted the prince and went on his quiet way. " There goes the only man I have ever envied and the man whose example I will follow," said Sidhartta to his companion. " All my wealth I will gladly give," he continued, " and all my honours willingly resign to be like him, free from all care, and to cherish a good hope of the brighter world." So saying, he entered the palace and began to make preparations as if for a journey.

When the night came and all the household was sunk in sleep, Sidhartta called Channa and bade him bring his horse Kantaka, the most beautiful and swiftest steed in the royal stables. While Channa was absent on this mission the prince entered his father's chamber and kissed him softly, so that he might not arouse him, a last good-night. Then he mounted his horse, and Channa, swift of foot as a deer, bounded along by his side with his hand upon Kantaka's mane. The guards were struck with terror at the sight of the large white horse and the royal figure that bestrode him and the vaulting attendant by his side. They gave way and fled as Sidhartta rode forward. Then he came to the city gates and Kantaka was preparing to over-leap the tall iron barriers when suddenly they flew open of their own accord. Now, through fields and woods he had never seen before, over rough roads, past miserable huts and places of wailing and yards where the dead lay buried, the fugitive prince rode, not sorrowfully as Channa thought, but rejoicing that he had escaped from a charmed life of deception into one that, spite of its miseries and horrors, was real and true. " There is much work to be done in a world like this," he said to his faithful companion. And Channa answered, " Ah, Lord, all the work of all the men in the world will not make it worth living in forever." " True," replied Sidhartta, " but it can be made less sorrowful, and with the knowledge of the world beyond it may be made a place of hope and peace. This shall be my work." When the day dawned, many long miles separated the fugitives from the city of Kapila. Then Sidhartta stopped and dismounted from his horse. He took off his royal raiment and put on a coarse gown that he had carried in a bundle behind him. Then he took his sword and with its sharp edge cut his long hair close to his head. The sword and all his princely attire he gave to Channa, saying, " Mount Kantaka and take these things back to Kapila to my father. Tell him that I have gone to live the better life here and to seek the best which is hereafter. Give him his son's love and gratitude for all his intended kindness and let him know that all the treasures in the world will not tempt me back again." Channa was loath to go, for he wanted to share his master's life. He begged to accompany Sidhartta, but the prince said " No, go and bear this message, and afterwards you may do as I have done." Then Channa tried to mount Kantaka, but the faithful horse would not suffer him. Again and again he tried him with caressing words, but all in vain. The dumb servant looked after his master who was walking along the dusty road in his homely dress with the alms-bowl in his hand like a beggar. Kantaka neighed loudly to attract his attention, but the prince never turned or gave the slightest sign that he had heard the faithful creature's cry. Then a great convulsion passed through Kantaka's body and he fell dead to the ground. Sadly Channa took up the prince's dress and ornaments together with his sword, and walked back alone to the royal city of Kapila.

There was consternation and dire dismay in the palace when Sidhartta's departure was known ; and, when Channa arrived days afterwards, a weary, sad-hearted, travel stained man, and told his story, Sudhodana's grief knew no bounds. He sent out proclamations to all the kings of India offering them rich rewards if they would induce his son to come back to his realm and his father's embrace. He dispatched messengers from the royal household along all roads, charging them that, if they could do it without harm to his son, they should bring him back. Meanwhile Sidhartta went forward. By day he begged his food from door to door and told the people who received him of the new life, and by night he lay down anywhere in fields, by the roadside, or in the jungle, where the wild beasts did him no harm. Thus he travelled many hundreds of miles, passed on the

way by his father's messengers who did not know
him, till he came to the great city of Rajagriha.   It was
then a city of palaces surrounded by five hills, near which
flowed tributary streams of the great river Ganges.   There
was no such city in all the rich kingdom of Bahar.   Sidhartta
entered the city and begged from house to house, everywhere speaking gently of the new life in which there should
be neither old age nor disease nor death, and where joys
should never end.   The people marvelled that so poor a
man should be so happy, and that one, who knew not where
his next meal would come from, should be so free from all
care and anxiety.   The king Vimbasara heard of the recluse
and learned that his lodging was the shadow of a rock outside of the city.   Thinking this might be the prince
Sidhartta, he visited the mendicant, and in his conversation
with him found that his guess was true.   Thereupon he
took him to a hill and showed him Rajagriha and many
hundred towns and villages beside.   " All these are mine,"
he said, " and so are the kingdoms of Anga and Magadha
far beyond the eye, kingdoms which bring me in great
wealth.   Come and be my partner on the throne, to share
the possession of this great empire."   But Sidhartta replied, " Frailty and sorrow and death are here.   I want no
earthly kingdom, but one from which these shall be forever
banished."   So the king left him and Sidhartta went on his
way.

Now the life of Sidhartta after this, with some things that
are true and good, and alas, very, very many that are foolish and heathenish, you may read some day in the Buddhist
books.   After he had travelled over much of India, teaching the people to live better lives and kill no living thing, to
give up war and all that might injure others, and to do

everything with a view to the life that lies beyond, the time of his death came. He had travelled with his faithful cousin and follower, Ananda, over the northern mountains into the country of Nepaul. When he reached the city of Kusinara his strength failed him, and he said, "Ananda, I am weary; let us rest;" then laid him down to die. Many came to visit him and hear his last words which were these: "Keep my precepts, for I depart to the land where there is no old age, no sickness, no death, and where joys bring no sorrow." This Sidhartta is the Buddha that half of the people of Asia worship to-day.

————

Well, do I wish you to be like this Indian prince? God forbid. I would have you be as noble as he was in seeking to know what is real and true; as brave as he was in facing all the sad sights, the trouble and sorrow that are in the world; as earnest as he was in persistently overcoming all obstacles in the way of finding a better world; as self-deny-ing in giving up earthly things for the sake of the heavenly. And I would have you be, like him, missionaries to go out into the world even as poor teachers of religion, dependent upon the gifts of those you teach, that you may impart the true knowledge of earth and heaven which you have gained. But the story of Sidhartta fails in this that it does not tell us what is the ground of peace and holy living here, nor show us our title to the blessed life hereafter. Sidhartta threw away his father's idols, but he had no God to put in their place. You have the maker of the universe, the God that is very near since in Him we all live and move and have our being, the Father who is in heaven. To Him belongs the deathless world, the sorrowless sinless world you seek. The

prince of Kapila had no saviour but himself, for by his own
sufferings his followers pretend that he paid the penalty of
his sins and by his own good deeds they say he deserved
the better life. And we know, for our hearts condemn us,
that no sufferings of ours can take away sin, and that our
best and purest actions are not worthy to be named before
the God of holiness. The Buddhists know this to-day, if
they would but confess it, for they make Buddha or Sidhartta their saviour in their prayers. You have a Saviour
from death who is the Prince of Life ; a Saviour from sorrow,
who was the Man of Sorrows and the first Comforter, for the
Holy Ghost was called by Him " another Comforter " ; a
Saviour, above all, from sin which is the cause of every evil,
for, though sinless and holy, " He was made sin for us that
we might be made the righteousness of God in Him." The
good Christian life you lead is not, like that of Sidhartta, one
of mere selfish seeking after the bliss of heaven, a piling up
of good works or merit against the day of account : but it is
following Jesus Christ, it is doing the will of the Father,
it is loving the brethren as our God loved and still loves us,
it is working out what God's grace works in, pouring forth
with a free full heart that treasure of Christ which the Holy
Ghost causes to flow from the throne of heaven into our
empty souls. It is very marvellous that the Indian prince
should have found so much truth, and that the truth he
found should have conquered the darkness of heathen idol-
atry in so many lands. How great then should be the vic-
tories of that fuller, perfect truth which God has revealed
through the ages, not to one man but to many, whose crown-
ing glory is the cross of His own son ! If Buddhism ever
shone with the semblance of fine gold it has long ages since
became very dim, and so degraded is that creed to-day that

the very heathen point the finger of scorn at the lazy, super-
stitious, and often immoral priests, who pretend to be followers of the son of Sudhodana. It has not raised a single
nation in the scale of righteousness, intelligence, and true
humanity. A poet has called it the light of Asia ; but, outside
of the story of Sidhartta's life, not even history can tell us of
a people whom it made happy and good. Then let us thank
God for all that He teaches us ; for all that He enables us
to learn, in our minds, by the use of the powers He has
given, and above all by His Holy Word and Spirit ; thank
Him for what is good in Sidhartta's life and doctrine, and in
those of all the world's teachers ; but let us bless Him for
the mercy which gave to us " the shining light, that shineth
more and more unto the perfect day." This we will learn
from Sidhartta's story, " Love not the world, neither the
things that are in the world. The world passeth away and
the lust thereof : but he that doeth the will of God abideth
forever."

■

The Peruvian Brothers.

■

The Peruvian Brothers.

"And the light shineth in darkness, and the darkness comprehended it not."—JOHN I. 5.

The southern part of Peru, where Potosi stands the highest city in the world, and the neighboring parts of the great empire of Brazil are rich in silver and gold and precious gems. In the old days, when the Indians had these countries to themselves, they used to wash the gold out of the river sands and pick lumps of silver off the mountain sides. Thus they found plenty for all their wants, and stored up enough to make the Spaniards, who took their country from them, very rich. But when these Spaniards learned where their Indian subjects had got the silver and gold and had seen the places with their own eyes, they were not content to wash the sands and pick up loose pieces of precious metal from the surface of the ground. They made up their minds to dig into the heart of the mountains and into the depths of the earth for what they seemed to love better than all things beside. Not with their own hands did they do this work, but by those of the poor Peruvians whom they robbed of their liberty as well as of their land. So thousands of the natives were armed with pickaxe, spade, and crowbar, and sent to make mines, to dig great pits in the ground, and cut out long tunnels and passages stretching in every direction where there was a sign that treasures might be found.

When these first began their work they saw the light of day
shining down upon them, but, as they went on making the
tnnnels long, they came to a region of thick darkness where
torches and lamps were their only guides.   The carriers
brought the ore to the foot of the mine and often caught a
glimpse of sunlight, but those who worked with pick and
spade and those who piled the loads far in the bowels of the
earth had to content themselves with the dismal flicker of
the lamps by night and by day alike.   There were soldiers
on guard at the entrance to the mine and overseers keeping
watch below continually, so that no one of the captive workmen might escape from his life of toil and slavery.

Among those who were carried away from their homes
to work in the mines was an Indian named Topa-Curi,
whose forefathers had been kings but who now, like
all his countrymen, was very poor.   When he was taken
away, his wife, Mama-Micay, prayed that she might be
allowed to go with her husband and to take with her
their two infant boys, Huascar and Titu.   Whether the
overseer was a kind man, or whether he thought that he
might get some work out of the wife and more work out
of the husband by giving her this permission, we cannot
say, but Mama-Micay was allowed to go and bury herself in
the mine where Topa-Curi laboured.   She said good-bye to
the sunlight and the fields, carried her little children down
the steep, long ladders, and, after what seemed the longest
journey she had ever taken in her life, came to the place in
the darkness which was henceforth to be her home.   The
babies were too young to know anything of the bright world
they had left behind them, yet only when she thought of
them did the fond mother and loving wife regret that she
had made such a choice.

It was a weary life, that of the mine. Years and weeks and days were all alike, nor indeed could the labourers tell when it was day and when night, for there was nothing to distinguish them. But Mama-Micay cheered her husband at his toil, and often did they snatch a few hours that should have been spent in sleep, to watch with fond eyes their children at play. As these grew up, their father and mother spoke much to the boys and tried to teach them other things than those they saw in the mine. They told them of the fresh, clear air and the healthful winds that blow from one end of heaven to the other ; of the wide expanse of field and plain, of the green grass, the trees and flowers, of the sportive llamas that played like goats upon the mountain sides, of the brilliant plumage of the birds and the thousands of busy insects that filled the world with life. But most of all they tried to make them know the great vaulted sky overhead, so far above that no eye could reach its blue depths, and stretching away on every side till it was lost to sight in the long, long distance. They told the boys of the lights of that sky and of the earth beneath, of the bright sun that rose in early morning among rosy clouds and filled the world all day with his golden radiance till he sank at night in the purple west, and then of the pale lady moon and all her glittering train of stars lighting up the dimness between sunset and sunrise again.

The boys listened eagerly to all that was told them, but they did not understand. They had never seen since they began to think anything but the black mine and the grimy workers, the shining metal and the smoky lamps. When they tried to picture to themselves the sun and moon and stars, they only saw some round things a little brighter than silver and not so yellow and smoky as the lamps. Of the wide earth and sky they could form no picture at all, since they had never seen anything but narrow passages walled all around with solid earth and stone. Bats and mice they had seen, and besides human beings they were the only living things which helped them to think of the busy and beautiful life above. Topa-Curi and Mama-Micay almost gave up in despair their efforts to teach the children about the world to which they belonged, when they saw how impossible it was for them to understand something the like of which they had never seen. They begged the carriers to bring a flower, a leaf, a blade of grass, or an insect from the mouth of the mine, anything that belonged to the upper world, and with these they tried to teach the boys instead of teaching them by words. The boys handled the living things and examined them by the light of the miners' lamps, wondering much at what they saw. Huascar seemed to understand, and showed that he did by wishing earnestly to go to the place from which the flowers came, but Titu, when they faded in the sickly air of the mine and lost their beauty, threw them away, and went to play among the heaps of broken rock and stones.

The two brothers had grown to be big boys. The overseer of the gallery in which their father and mother worked saw them, and said they must work also for their daily bread. So they helped their mother to pile the ore out of the rock into the baskets in which it was carried away. They noticed that she needed all their help and did not seem able to work as she had done ; and one day or night, for they could not tell which it was, after the overseer had spoken roughly to her because she was so slow and she had tried to labour as before, she suddenly staggered and fell to the ground. Topa-Curi carried his senseless wife

away to the little corner which was all their home, and he
and the boys stayed with her for the few hours she lived.
Many things she said, but most of all her sayings were to
the children, that they should find and live in the light of
day. So she died, and, while broken-hearted Topa-Curi
went back to his toil, the strange hands of the carriers
placed her dead body upon their loads and bore it away to
the mouth of the mine. Then for the first time since
Mama-Micay had entered her living tomb the light of
heaven shone upon her, but received no answer from the
sightless eyes; the warm sun's rays fell upon her cheek but
it was cold in death.

It was not long till Topa-Curi followed his wife. In his
last illness, which was very short and the only one that
gained him rest from labour, he spoke much to his boys of
the world above ground. Again with his feeble breath he
worked hard to make them understand what daylight is,
and told them in a whisper, so that none might hear, of
something he had seen. One day working in another gallery, which was now deserted because the ore failed, he
had seen far away a little patch of white clear light which
he knew must be the light of heaven, the light of the sun.
He told the boys how to find this gallery, and besought
them earnestly, for their own good, to put forth all their
strength to make that light their own. " Don't believe in
any light you find here," he said; " the true light is that
which shines from without." Then Huascar and Titu were
left alone, two motherless, fatherless orphans, to toil in the
gloomy mine which had killed their parents. Some of the
enslaved miners were kind to them, because their father and
mother had been gentle and good and had come of a royal
race, but others behaved very differently towards the

brothers because they had been cruelly treated themselves, and Spanish brutality had almost made them brutes. Yet with these poor people, good or bad, kind or unkind, they had to live, to work with them when the overseer said it was day, to sleep with them when he called it night.

The boys had always been different in their characters and ways, even while their parents were alive and taught them the same lessons. Now that their parents were gone, the difference was more marked. Huascar liked to be much alone that he might think of what had been told him, and when he sought the company of others it was that of those who loved to speak of his father and mother whose friends they were. Titu wished to be friends with everybody. He was in the mine, and he was going to make the best of it. Though not so good a workman as Huascar he managed to please the overseer, and by agreeing with all that the worthless miners said, even when they half ridiculed his dead parents, he kept on good terms with them. Of the upper world he never thought, but he longed to find some treasure in the mine. Often Huascar would call him aside and ask him if he remembered the counsels of his dying mother and father, and if he were willing to go with him in search of the light. Titu did not remember much, for, though he grieved over the death of his best friends, he had not paid great attention to their words. But he said that he was willing and as anxious as Huascar to go in search of the light. So they agreed that while their companions were sleeping they would explore the deserted galleries of the mine.

Before the boys could go forth to their search they had to provide themselves with light for the way. The lamps they could not take, for these were fastened to the walls and pillars and would be missed at once even if they could be removed. But torches were used for occasional visits to the dark galleries and many of them had been tossed aside when only half burned. So, watching their chance, Huascar and Titu gathered a number of these half-burned torches and laid them together in a dark and secret place. Then one night quietly they rose from the sides of their sleeping neighbours, and brought some torches from the hiding place. Tremblingly, for fear of being seen, they lit one at the most distant lamp and hurried noiselessly towards the deserted tunnel. That night they found nothing, nor the next, nor the next again. But every night they went farther and farther, until they knew the ground so well that, but for the sake of finding something new, they could have gone over it in the dark. They were wise enough also to leave torches all along the way as far as they had gone, to help them in future search.

One day they were nearly discovered. The Spanish governor with his wife and many attendants, all richly dressed and ornamented, came to see the mine. They walked through the lighted galleries where they could see the work going on. Pieces of silver were struck from the rock and handed to them. They even spoke to the slaves about their life, and, as the overseers and masters of the mine were looking on, these poor creatures were obliged to say nothing of its hardships and misery. Then the governor asked if there was anything more to see and was told about the deserted tunnels. The ladies all wished to see these, so the overseer called Huascar and Titu, with two other lads, and bade them take torches and go on before the party. With fear and trembling Huascar and Titu went forward, trying all the way to prevent anyone seeing the half-burned torches they had laid here and there along the road, and pretending not to know the way in which they were going. But nobody noticed anything; the overseer was quite satisfied; and the haughty governor's lady even thanked the boys for lighting up the darkness before her. Then the party went back again to the welcome light of the sun, and the dreary life of the mine went on as before.

Huascar was happy that night. One of the ladies whose face had pleased him the best had let a flower fall out of her hand on the way. Huascar had picked up the flower and handed it to her, but she had said, "Keep it boy; you don't see many flowers here; they don't grow in these dismal mines." So Huascar kept the flower, a lovely blossom pure waxy white with shining dark green leaves and such a delicate perfume that it filled his heart with joy, and made his longing tenfold greater to return to the world from which it had come. He fell asleep with the flower upon his breast and dreamed sweet dreams of light and beauty. Titu was awake. He could not sleep. He had not received anything, but his eye had caught a gleam of light as he had carried his torch along the dark corridors. What was it? He resolved to find out and to find out alone. Let Huascar sleep with his worthless flower; he would find the light his father and mother had spoken of so often, and would perhaps allow his brother to see it in his hands. He went away in the darkness, for he knew the road and feared to light a torch lest he might be surprised and lose his treasure. Groping his way along the silent deserted galleries, keeping his eyes fixed upon the ground, he came at length near the spot where he had seen the gleam. Yes, there it was; he saw the same gleam before him. And, as he went forward, it shone brighter with a thin clear beautiful light, all unlike the yellow flare of lamp and torch. He knelt beside it and saw that it was not one light but many, though two were larger and brighter than all the others. He put his hand over them to feel if they could burn, but no, the lights were cold. He touched them ; they were hard as stone. He picked one up and all the others came with it and sparkled over his hand. He gazed upon his treasures and muttered joyfully to himself, " I have found the lights, the sun and moon and stars ; I am in the world that my father and mother told me to seek." They shed light on his hands, these gems, but none upon his path. Again and again, as he looked at them, he struck his head and feet against the ragged walls of the gallery, and when he reached his brother's side both head and feet were bleeding with many a wound. Still his treasure comforted him as he placed it carefully in his bosom and covered it with his rags for fear that any eye might catch its gleam. And all this time Huascar lay with the sweet flower all exposed upon his breast and a smile of quiet gladness on his half-parted lips.

When the voice of the overseer called them to work, the two boys arose, Huascar refreshed and cheerful, Titu tired and sullen. The flower which Huascar carried had begun to droop, but its fragrance seemed to be even sweeter than before. Titu's diamonds, for such they were, did him no good, for their light was hidden in the folds of his ragged clothes, and a great fear was in his heart lest they should be taken from him. When night came he was too weary for the search that Huascar proposed, but, when he thought his brother was asleep, he stole away to the entrance of the first deserted gallery, and there sat down in the darkness to look at his treasures. Soon he heard the sound of footsteps

falling quietly, and his heart almost stopped beating, so terrified was he at the thought of being found out. He lay
very quiet, however, and at last was overjoyed to hear a
voice which he knew well, softly calling "Titu, where are
you?" Titu answered as softly, and then Huascar came
and sat down by his side. Titu said "We need not search
any more for the sun and moon and stars, for I have found
them." So he took the diamonds out of their wrappings
and showed them to his brother sparkling upon his hand.
But he was disappointed to see that their light was paler
and thinner than it was the night before, although he did
not tell this to Huascar. "There," he said, pointing to the
largest, "is the sun, and this is the moon, and these little
ones are the stars, for their light is quite different from the
lights of the mine, and no one needs to light them because
they are always shining." Huascar answered, "O my poor
brother, these are not what our father and mother told us
about. I don't know what they are, though they are very
beautiful; but if they were the sun and moon and stars
they would show us the flowers and the living creatures and
the great wide earth and sky. Do you not remember how
our father said :—Don't believe in any light you find here;
for the true light shines from without? Let us still go in
search of that light?" But Titu would not. He insisted
that he had found what his parents had bidden him seek
for, and that these shining things were enough to make him
happy. Then he looked at the diamonds again, and
pressed their cold hard sides to his cheeks and lips, as if to
thank them that they had come to lighten his darkness.
After this the two brothers stole back quietly to their
wretched bed and fell asleep.

Next day there was a great commotion in the mine. The

chief officer was there and by his side walked a gaily-dressed soldier, one of the Governor's aids. They visited all the galleries and passages and carefully searched those through which the Governor's party had passed two days before. When they found nothing, they told the overseers to let all the workmen know that the Governor's lady had lost her diamond bracelet of great value somewhere in the mine, and that whoever found it would be richly rewarded if he were a freeman, and if he were a slave would receive his liberty. As soon as this was made known, everybody was eager to begin the search except the two brothers. One of them knew where it was and rejoiced in the thought that it would buy his brother's freedom ; the other had it wrapped up in his rags and trembled to think that it might be taken away. While they were together, pretending to help their companions in the search, Huascar begged Titu to give the bracelet to the chief officer who was still not far away, and gain his liberty. He tried to make him understand how beautiful was the world into which this liberty would bring him, and prayed him for his mother's sake to take advantage of his great good fortune, and by it win something better still. But poor Titu would not listen. He said he had no bracelet, but the sun and moon and stars, and these he would give up to nobody. So for fear that the people would suspect them if they talked too long together, Huascar left his brother and went on as far as he could into the dark galleries.

The diamond bracelet was not found that day. When all the seekers came back empty-handed, Huascar heard the chief officer instruct the overseers to question every man, woman, and child in the mines about it early the next morning, and to have them thoroughly searched lest it

should be hidden in their clothing. Then Huascar knew
that nothing could save his brother, for instead of a reward
he would be severely punished and perhaps put to death,
for the law was then very cruel towards thieves who were
slaves. He went to Titu, and with tears in his eyes told
what he had heard, and of the dreadful fate which awaited
him. Titu was frightened, but he would not part with his
treasure. Already he had told a lie in saying to the overseer, when he returned from the search, that he had found
nothing. Now he resolved to go and hide the diamonds in
a place where nobody would dream of looking. Huascar
reasoned with him a long time, but all to no effect. Then
he sorrowfully turned away, only a little comforted to think
that at least he had warned his brother and saved his life.

That night Titu went away as early as possible along the
deserted galleries with his treasure. He went without a light,
for he knew the way even better than when he found his
treasure, and came at last to a place near where two galleries
met in the form of a cross. There, all unsuspecting, he sat
down to look at his shining stones before putting them away
in a crevice of the rock just above his head. He fondled
them as if they were alive, and bent his head over them to
admire their fading brilliance amid the darkness. Suddenly
he heard a foot-fall. " It is that meddling Huascar," he said
to himself, for he could see no light and knew that only he
and his brother could get on without one. So he remained
as he was, sitting on the ground with the diamonds still in
his lap, when in a moment the light of a torch flashed upon
him round the corner of the cross gallery, and in another
instant a man's strong clutch was at his throat. He knew
the man to be one of the worst in all the mine, and yet Titu
thought he had made him his friend. " Give me that

bracelet !" said the man, as he still kept his hand upon the boy's throat and with the other held the torch near his face. Titu wrenched himself away and said " I have no bracelet, but the sun, moon and stars that my father and mother bade me seek long ago, and these I will never give up." " You are a little fool," answered the wicked fellow, " and your parents were fools before you. That is the noble lady's diamond bracelet, and you must give it me at once, for before morning it must win me my freedom." Titu turned to run, but in a moment his enemy was upon him again. The boy struggled bravely and the man held on firmly, for he too was striving for a great boon. His torch he allowed to fall on the ground, so that, with two hands free, he might be better able to rob the lad of his treasure. But Titu clutched it in his grasp and all the strong man's power could not wrench the bracelet away. Maddened at last by the boy's courage and stubbornness, he lifted him in his arms and dashed him with all his force against the rocky wall, not once only but again and again. Then he laid the senseless body on the ground and, opening the limp fingers, took away the prize for which the boy had given his young life. Then he went to pick up his torch, but during the contest it had burned away rapidly along its whole length, and now there was no place by which it could be held. With a curse upon the boy and another on the torch he hastened as fast as he could in the darkness towards the inhabited part of the mine.

In the meanwhile Huascar lay awake, wondering why his brother staid away so long. He feared that some of the workmen suspected them, and especially one who, on account of his wickedness, was nicknamed Supay, a Peruvian word that means " the evil spirit." What was his horror, then, when he looked over the forms of his sleeping companions and saw that Supay's place was vacant. Hardly knowing what he did, he arose and hurried along the galleries in search of his brother. He had not gone very far when he heard rapid footsteps coming nearer at every moment, until at last with a loud cry a man struck against his outstretched hand, and with chattering teeth rushed past him. It was a man, not Titu, he knew, and perhaps it was Supay. Faster and faster Huascar went on till he saw the smouldering torch upon the ground, and beside it the body of his brother. He raised the body in his arms and spoke to Titu, but got no answer. He saw that it was covered with blood, the poor head terribly bruised, the eyes fixed and staring. Then he knew the truth: Titu was dead and Supay had killed him. Alas! that brother whom he loved so well even in death, he could do nothing for him, could not even dig his grave in the hard rocky mine. Oh! if he had only been more diligent, if he had found the true light, this terrible thing would not have happened! Then he laid his brother's body quietly down, wiped the blood from his face, folded the lifeless arms upon his breast, and kissed Titu his last good-night.

Huascar found a torch and lit it at the embers of the one which Supay had dropped. Then away he went along the gallery his father had told him of, seeking for the light not on the ground but overhead. He came at last to the end of the long passage. It did not end in a level wall like others he had seen, but the floor seemed to rise step by step till, not far from the height of the roof, a low, narrow opening appeared half blocked up with loose stones and masses of rock. These he tore away and gently placed upon the steps below, thrusting the end of his torch into a crack in the floor to leave both hands free for the work. All the time he kept his eye fixed upon a greyish streak which he saw between the stones, and in which he thought once or twice that he could notice a little golden twinkle. His torch was burning down quickly and he was sure that the overseers were calling the miners to work, but they were still far away from him, and between lay his murdered brother. The gray streak changed ; it became a dull-red colour, and then turned into bright gold, but still it was only a streak between two great stones. He reached these stones at length, but they would not move. Then he gave one a push outwards to loosen it ; suddenly it rolled away from his hands, the golden glory of the morning light filled its place, and for the first time fell upon Huascar's conscious eyes.

There was no time for delay. Huascar heard the sound of voices and of heavy feet resounding through the echoing galleries. They were far away yet, but every moment would bring them nearer. How glad he was that the stone, too heavy for him to lift or guide, had rolled outwards and not in. Hastily he scrambled on hands and knees through the opening, came out into the light of day, and then, all dazzled by its splendour and exhausted by his labours, fell fainting to the ground and rolled some yards down the mountain side. The overseers did not find him nor even the passage by which he escaped. They only found the dead body of poor Titu and knew that he had been murdered. When Huascar came out of his faint and opened his eyes, he saw all that his parents had told him, such a beautiful fairy land as he never had dreamed of even in his brightest dreams. But he saw more than the wide earth and over-arching sky, the glorious sun that his forefathers used to worship as a god, and the blue rivers in the valleys in which he was reflected as in a mirror. There was an aged man bending over him, a man with silvery hair and kindly face, dressed in a long black robe,

16

who looked as if he loved the boy.   As Huascar had never
seen anyone but Topa-Curi whose gaze was so tender and
kind, he lifted up his hands to the aged stranger and said " My
father." The old priest answered, ·' My poor boy, you could
not have spoken better ; come with me and I will be your
father." Then Huascar arose and leaning on his new father's
arm walked down the mountain side through the beautiful
summer morning to his home.

He wanted nothing now but food enough to keep him
alive, for his soul was filled and more than satisfied with the
new world he had found.   True, he would fain have had his
father and mother there, although the old priest told him they
were in a better place ; and Titu, yes, he would willingly
have remained a slave forever, if Titu could only have enjoyed
this blessed life in his stead.   But he must sit at the priest's
table, and, though it bore humble fare, it was princely in
Huascar's judgment and to his taste compared with that of
the mine.   New clothes too he must have, and so the old
ones must be taken off and thrown away.   When the clean
light summer dress came, and Huascar threw off his dirty
rags which he had worn so many years that he might put it
on, something that had lain in his breast fell to the ground.
He thought it was only a piece of stone that had found its
way there while he was creeping through the opening by
which he escaped. But the old priest's eye fell upon it and he
picked it up ; it was the diamond bracelet.   The murderer,
Supay, carrying it in his hand had flung it unwittingly from
him in his fright at meeting Huascar, and there in the bosom
of his coarse shirt it had lain ever since.   The priest asked
him whence it came, and Huascar told him all the sad story
of his brother's delusion and dreadful death.

The boy slept all night in a comfortable bed, and a pleasant, restful sleep it was. In the morning he awoke with the singing of the birds, and hurried out into the pleasant light of day to gather wayside flowers. That day he took the old priest's hand, and together they went in search of a carriage. When they had found one they travelled in it along level roads, past fields and woods and by rocky mountain sides, till they came to the Governor's palace. The Governor knew the priest and respected him for his goodness, so that he did not delay seeing him when he called. The priest gave him the diamond bracelet and told him all the story which he had learned from Huascar. Then the Governor spoke kindly to Huascar, who trembled for fear that he would be sent back to the darkness, and asked him many questions about his father and mother and the life of the mine and his dead brother Titu. The frightened boy answered all the questions so honestly and truthfully that the Governor turned to his old friend and said, " Train this good lad up for me. I will be at the expense of his education ; and when he is old enough he shall be my inspector of mines to save others from the terrible wrongs that he has known." So the old priest's heart was glad and Huascar's joy knew no bounds.

While they were talking, the Governor's lady with some ladies and officers of their court came in, because they had heard that the famous bracelet was found. Huascar had to tell his story over again, while all listened with great attention. When they heard how poor Titu mistook the diamonds for the sun, moon and stars, the officers and some of the ladies laughed heartily, but the Governor did not laugh, nor his lady, nor she who had given Huascar the flower ; and the old priest said, " It is the saddest thing I have ever known, although something like it happens every day." .The ladies answered, " How could the poor boy know any better,

seeing he never knew the light?"   But again the old priest
said, " Huascar never saw the light to know it, yet he knew
better. He was told, and he believed, that the light does not
lie in the darkness but shines down into it from above.   Thus
he found the blessed light and rejoices in it to-day."

Taught by the kind old priest who loved him as a son,
Huascar grew up to be a wise and good man.   The Governor
fulfilled his promise and made him inspector of mines.   He
saved the children by bringing them all up into the light of day,
and even the men and women were allowed, under his man-
agement, to leave their gloomy abodes when they wished and
enjoy the pleasures of the life above.   At the mouth of the
mine in which he had lived and toiled he placed a monument
over Titu's grave, on which were the words : " He never knew
the light of which he had been told ; and he died, because he
mistook the treasures of earth for the glory of heaven."

You may think it strange that boys should have been so
ignorant of the world we know so well as to have no idea of
the heavenly bodies and the green earth on which they shine.
Yet how many wise men even in this world are so shut up
by education and prejudice and ignorance of the word of
God that they have no notion of the true light which lighteth
every man that cometh into the world.   Those who find their
chief enjoyments in earthly things have their eyes blinded to
heavenly things.   Wealth and fame, art and science, all the
desirable things of this earth cannot lead into the light of
God's countenance or open the gate of that heaven where
there are pleasures for evermore.   They are merely play-
things, brilliant indeed with a lustre that comes from God
whose creatures they are and who gives us all things richly

to enjoy, but toys all the same. Sought after and used apart from God their very brilliancy fades, they become the causes of cares, jealousies, strifes, bloodshed and many other evils. The end of these things is death. Better grope all one's earthly life in the darkness of the world to find the light at last, than rest contentedly in the darkness admiring the feeble gleam of some worldly treasure. But we need not grope so long. " He that seeketh findeth," said the Light of men. It was He also who said, " He that doeth truth cometh to the light." The one lad of the story did truth, the other did not. The first believed the story of his parents who had seen the light ; the second was wise in his own conceit. Let us then believe the record that God has given and act according to that belief. This is doing truth. That record is confirmed by numberless witnesses whose voices are all round about us in the page of history and the book of nature, in the society of our friends and the teachings of our own consciences. All direct us towards Him who said, " I am the light of the world ; he that followeth me shall not walk in darkness but shall have the light of life." Find Christ, and in Him the light of God's countenance will be lifted up upon you, making this present world full of highest joy and opening broad views into the eternal glory.

■

XII.

The Island Kingdom.

The Island Kingdom.

"Lay up for yourselves treasures in heaven."—Matthew vi. 20.

Everybody who has read the Bible knows about the Red Sea which the Israelites crossed and where Pharoah and his host were drowned. Strange to say, some people who know very little about the Bible have stories that tell of this sea, stories which were carried by their fathers, hundreds and hundreds of years ago, from an old far off home in the east. In the mountain range of the Pyrenees between France and Spain live the Basques, a strange people, who speak a language unlike any other that is spoken in Europe. They have many old tales which have come down to those who are now living from a time when the Basques had no Bible and when they worshipped heathen gods. Some of these stories are about the Red Sea and its wonderful islands ever green and fair, and their enchanted cities with walls of brass and palaces of gold. But none of these stories are as wonderful or as true as the Jewish one I am going to tell.

The Red Sea begins at the south between Abyssinia in Africa and the great country of Arabia, where it meets the Indian ocean. It runs upwards between Egypt and Arabia till it comes to a place not very far to the south of Palestine, where a three cornered piece of rocky land juts out and seems to stop the way. This three cornered peninsula is the land of Sinai where the children of Israel wandered forty years and where God gave the law to Moses. It divides the Red Sea into two long gulfs, one of which runs up into Egypt, and the other, into Arabia. The one that borders the land of Egypt is called the Gulf of Suez and is the branch of the Red Sea which Moses and the Israelites crossed. And the other, between Sinai and Arabia, now called the Gulf of Akaba, is the one to which my story belongs. At the head of this gulf there were in the old days two seaport towns called Elath and Ezion-geber. So famous was the first of these that it used to give name to the gulf itself, which was called the Gulf of Elath. We do not know who built these towns, but for a long time they were in the possession of the Edomites, whose first father was Esau the son of Isaac. King David of Israel drove the Edomites out and took the towns to himself. His son Solomon built many ships in them, ships that sailed for him to Arabia and Ethiopia and far away into the Indian ocean, some people think even beyond India, bringing back gold and silver, precious woods and stones, ivory and apes and peacocks. Sixty years after Solomon was dead, Jehoshaphat, a good prince, became king of Judah, while the wicked Ahab ruled over Israel. He also built a fleet, but a great storm arose at Ezion-geber which dashed his ships upon a rocky reef just outside of the harbour, so that they could not go in search of gold When Jehoshaphat died, his wicked son Jehoram took his place. He had married a heathen wife, the daughter of Ahab, and tried to make the Jews worshippers of the idols which his queen served. So God's hand was taken away from him and the Edomites rebelled and got back the seaport towns which David had captured a hundred and fifty years before. Eighty years the Edomites kept the gates of the sea, and then another good king of the Jews, named Uzziah, defeated them in battle and became master of Elath, which he built up and made stronger than ever. But he loved war and farming better than the free life of the sea, so that there was no great sending out of ships in his day. Ahaz, the grandson of Jotham, was a wicked king. In his reign Rezin, the king of Syria, drove the Jews away from the sea, but he kept his conquest for a very short time. Tiglath Pileser, the great king of Assyria, came against him and killed him, so the gulf of Elath and its towns became part of the great Assyrian empire.

Now, in the old happy days when the Israelites were masters of Elath, many rich merchants dwelt there. The chief of them was one Abiad to whom all the others were subject, because of his great wealth and remarkable wisdom. He had many servants in his employ who waited in his house, tilled his land, built his ships, and sailed to distant lands in his service. But among them all there was one whom he loved as a son, although he was young and had never been tried with great labours. His name was Benadam. Why Abiad should have chosen Benadam above all his other servants no one can tell, but certain it is that the rich merchant dearly loved the young man and was willing to do great things for him. One day he called the servant to him and said, "Benadam, I give you your freedom, and, as your freedom would be useless to you alone, I give you with it a ship in which you may go to distant lands and trade and gain great treasures. All you gain will be your own. All that I ask is that you will come and see one who loves you as a father loves his son and tell him of your success that he may rejoice with you in it." Benadam was full of joy at the tidings. He went down to the harbour of Elath and saw the

ship which his master had so generously given him. There
was no such beautiful vessel in all Abiad's fleet. With her
sharp prow and sloping masts and snowy sails, her seats for
a hundred rowers, her gem of a cabin, and deep hull able to
hold a great deal of treasure, it was the finest merchant-
man in all the harbour. A well trained crew manned the
ship and were kept in strict discipline by the captain, whose
name was Deror. Benadam was at first a little afraid of
Deror. He was very confident and bold but he did not
seem to know very much. All the sailors had to obey him,
although some of them did so in a very grudging way, as if
they were not sure that his orders were the best. However,
when the new owner of the vessel and Captain Deror came
to talk with each other, Benadam's doubts were removed,
and he thought he had got a very clever and brave man for
chief officer of his ship. If he had only noticed Hosah the
helmsman, he would have seen that he had no confidence
in the captain ; but although he knew that Hosah was a
good pilot and that Abiad esteemed him very highly, Benadam never dreamed of preferring his opinion to that of his
new friend Deror.

On a pleasant morning the ship left the harbour, bound
on a trading voyage to distant lands. The good merchant
Abiad came down to see Benadam off, and gave him
at parting charts of the Red Sea and the Indian Ocean beyond. " Study these charts with Deror," he said, " and
see that Hosah, or whoever else is helmsman, steers the ship
according to the courses laid down in them." Then he embraced his former slave and returned to the town. There
was not room enough to sail out of the port, so the rowers
took their places on the thwarts and pulled lustily at the
long sweeps till the vessel, large as she was, glided onwards

like a living thing towards the open water. When the rocks and shoals were passed and the way seemed clear and when the favouring breeze blew gently, the snowy sails were hoisted with much shouting and noise and the brave ship bore away for the south. The voyage was a dangerous one. Many ships had perished while undertaking it, because of the great winds that blew down the gulf between the rocky shores, and the stormy waves they raised, and the sunken rocks and coral reefs which seemed to lie everywhere in the sailor's course. Yet it was very pleasant for Benadam as the vessel moved gently onwards under the skilful guidance of the pilot Hosah. On his right hand rose the rugged rocky piles of Sinai, and, on his left, the mountain range that skirts the great Arabian desert reared its peaks towards the sky. There was grandeur in the land scenery but very little quiet beauty. What was wanting in the land, however, the water supplied. Soon as the ship came near a shallow place in the sea Benadam felt as if he were in a garden, for the waters were dyed with colours of every hue from the coral insects and sponges and sea-weeds and many other living things of beautiful shape and tint which flourished beneath the salt waves. Sometimes the shoals were as green as a well kept grassy lawn; sometimes yellow, and then the sailors said that one of Solomon's fleets laden with gold had sunk there; and sometimes red as the roses of Sharon or the seeds of the promegranate, so that Benadam did not wonder at the name Red Sea.

Three days passed before the ship left the gulf and its crew found themselves in the broader waters of the sea. Looking back on the fourth day they saw the land of Sinai fading from sight, although the white limestone cliffs at its southern point still stood out in bright contrast with the deep

blue waters at their base.   On went the vessel past many
islands into broad open waters where all sight of land was
sometimes lost, and where, now and again, as it was necessary to tack in the one direction or the other, the land of the
Pharaohs or the great desert home of the Arabian came in
view.   The point at which Benadam wished to touch first of
all was a port in the Arabian land of Sheba, whose queen in
former days had come to hear the wisdom of Solomon.   But
Sheba was still a thousand miles away, and a thousand miles
was a long voyage for ships to make in these old times.
There was not much danger now from reefs and shoals, for
the sea was a hundred and fifty miles wide from shore to
shore, so that the pilot had plenty sea room.   Yet as he had
no compass, for that was not found out till ages later, and as
he had to trust to the sun by day and the stars by night for
his reckoning in the open water, he was generally careful to
keep in sight of land.   Still the favouring breeze from the
north continued to blow, and the rowers' backs and arms
were saved, while the sails carried Benadam and his fortunes
to the south.

Now as you near the land of Sheba the reefs become
dangerous and there are very many islands, and such is the
state of the sea down to the point where it glides into the
ocean through a narrow channel.   There in your maps you
will see how the shores of Arabia and Africa almost seem to
touch, as those of Western Africa and Europe do at the
Straits of Gibraltar.   A month had passed, and the ship was
nearing this place of danger.   Benadam had been examining
the charts which Abiad had given him, and so far Hosah,
the pilot, had been steering by their aid.   Now he called
Deror, the captain, and consulted with him and Hosah about
their future course.   As they were talking matters over, he

saw plainly that the captain did not like Hosah, and, moreover, that he took to himself the credit of all the safe sailing
so far, and wished to go forward as he pleased. Hosah
pointed to the chart and said—"There is the course which
Abiad has laid down for us. If we do not follow it, we will
strike upon these rocks and shoals which he has marked
dangerous. I will follow these instructions." Then Deror
was angry. He answered, "I am captain here, and you
must steer as I direct. Do you think that Abiad has given
me charge of the ship for the purpose of obeying you, a
pilot?" But Hosah replied gently, "I do not ask you to
follow my sayings, but the instructions of one who is wiser
than either of us. If we do not do so we must suffer."
Deror, however, would not listen to the pilot. He turned
to Benadam and asked him if he were not captain of the
ship, and if hitherto he had any reason to be dissatisfied
with the way in which it was managed. The captain was
bold and blustering; the pilot quiet and modest. So Benadam, although he felt that he was not doing right, yielded
to the bold man and told Hosah to obey the captain and
steer according to his will and wisdom. The pilot gave no
answer but sorrowfully turned to his helm and stood there
with the chart before his eyes.

Benadam entered his cabin, and, as he hoped soon to arrive
in port, began to arrange in his mind what goods he should
exchange with the people of Sheba, and what articles he would
obtain from them to take back to Elath on his return voyage.
While he was busily engaged in this work he heard angry
voices overhead and a trampling of feet as if men were struggling. Then he heard a heavy blow, as if some one were
struck with a deadly weapon, and a splash in the water that
sounded like a body falling into the sea, and, last of all but

hardly a moment later, a faint voice crying " Beware of Deror."
Then all was silent again save the voice of the captain calling
to his sailors to spread more sail. Benadam started from his
couch and ran on deck. " Where is Hosah ?" he asked.
Deror replied, " The stupid fellow has fallen overboard, which
is just as well, for he would not let go the helm and was going
to take us miles out of our way." Then Benadam knew that
Deror had struck the quiet pilot and had thrown him into
the sea. " Where are the charts?" he asked again, and the
captain answered, " Hosah must have taken them with him,
or they have been blown away by the wind." And truly the
wind had begun to blow fiercely. Already the waves were
tossing high. The sun had set and a dark night was coming on.
But, spite of all this, the wicked captain in his mad pride and
ignorance was setting more sail, although already the ship
was driving furiously through the water. Benadam was afraid.
He felt that he had been a coward to listen to Deror, that he
was guilty of the death of Hosah as well as the captain whom
he had placed over the faithful pilot. He ventured to say
a word or two to the man he had so foolishly honoured
about the risk of piling on fresh canvass, but Deror turned
upon him so savagely that all his cowardice came back again
and he only said " Well, do as you like." Then he went back
to his cabin and lay upon his couch, full of sad and gloomy
thoughts.

Benadam could not rest. He was thrown from his couch
by the violence of the waves, and with difficulty found something by which he might hold, as the ship rose and fell or
swayed from side to side in the surging waters. He could
hear the timbers creaking with the strain of the vessel's
motion, and the shriek of the wind through the shrouds, and
the ripping of the sails, and the washing of the seas that

swept the decks. One by one he heard the despairing cries of the sailors who were carried away by the boarding waves and engulfed in the terrible billows of the sea. Still, in spite of all his fears and the terrors of the moment, he had hopes of reaching port and of gaining great stores of merchandise. In the brief lulls in the storm Deror's voice fell upon his ear, now loud and imperious and madly defiant as if he were the ruler of the winds and waves, and then changing to a foolish chuckle or an idiotic laugh. But these lulls lasted only for a moment and in a short time ceased altogether. The storm increased, the waters poured into the cabin and drove Benadam on hands and knees to the deck. What a wild scene, what a picture of desolation met his eyes! Not a sailor was visible; only the captain at the helm, and he a raving madman. As he hung by the after mast Benadam saw the moon arise among clouds, and by its dim light beheld, straight in the vessel's course, a great black rock that dashed the waves into high fountains of foam and spray. He staggered back to the helm and tried to drag Deror away, but his fingers were benumbed with cold and fear. The mad captain struck his master to the deck, and in another minute there was a crash as if the heavens were falling or the earth had rent asunder. The vessel was broken into a thousand fragments, the rich stores of merchandize scattered on a hundred waves, the wicked Deror engulfed in his frantic pride, and Benadam cast a waif upon the tempestuous sea.

How he lived through that dreadful night he could never tell. No human being came to his help, no fragment of the wreck supported his fainting form, yet some unseen arm, able to go down into the great sea depths and strong enough to battle with the waves and billows that swept over him, upheld the ruined merchant. When he came to himself it

17

was broad day-light, and he lay all helpless on a gently
sloping beach of sand whose margin was washed by a softly
rippling tide. Raising his head to look abroad, Benadam saw
that he was on an island protected all around by coral reefs
which broke the violence of the sea, and that the island was
large and green and beautiful ; and as he looked towards its
centre where towers and pinnacles showed that there must
be a town, he saw, between it and the point where he was
lying, a long procession moving. As it came nearer he could
distinguish horsemen and chariots and a great company of
people on foot, clad in holiday raiment. He could hear the
music to the sound of which they were marching, and the
shouts of the people who cried " Long live the king !" Then
Benadam wondered why they were coming his way, and what
business the king could have at this point of sandy beach
where there was neither building nor ship nor harbour. They
were almost upon him now, and great was his shame as he
looked at himself and thought of the contrast between his rags
and helplessness and the pomp and state of the great procession. He tried to stagger to his feet as he could not hide
himself, to pray the king to do him no harm, but between his
fright and his weariness he fainted and fell insensible to the
ground.

While he was unconscious some richly dressed officers
came to Benadam, raised him gently from the sand, and laid
him on a couch they had brought with them. They took off
his tattered clothes, washed away the sand and sea-weed from
his face and body, and dressed him in a purple robe of soft
and costly fabric dyed with the famous Tyrian dye. They
poured wine into his lips and, when he opened his eyes
refreshed by it as if by a pleasant sleep, they set a crown of
pure gold upon his head and bowed the knee before him,

while all the people shouted " Long live the king !" The shipwrecked merchant felt as if he were dreaming a very happy
dream, but he knew that what he saw was real, so he ventured
to ask one of the noblemen. "Tell me, sir, where is the king,
that I may let him know who I am and how I came here !"
The nobleman answered respectfully " You, my lord, are the
king and we know no other ; we have been waiting for you
many days." " I am no king," replied Benadam ; " I am a
poor shipwrecked merchant who has lost all he had by his
own folly and wickedness." But the noblemen again bent the
knee, and the musicians began to play and the royal banners
to wave high in the air, while the people shouted louder than
ever " Long live the king, long live our new-found king !"
Then they led him to the royal chariot, soft with luxurious
cushions and dazzling with ornaments of gold and pearls,
where the two chief officers of state sat beside him. Other
chariots followed. The horsemen and musicians went on
before, and behind came the joyful people waving palm
branches as they went, and ever proclaiming him their new-
found king.

Soon the procession reached the city and was met by more
people and officers of state, all eager to greet the king.
Benadam was brought to the royal palace and lodged
there in true royal fashion. Everything he desired was
set before him, and treasures of every description poured
into his palace gates. The people toiled cheerfully at their
daily tasks, cultivating the cornfields and vineyards, gathering
in the uncultivated places the myrrh and balsam and frankin-
cense that flows like sap out of the fragrant trees and shrubs
or forms like gum upon their surface, and trading to distant
lands for vessels of silver and gold and brass, of glass and
porcelain, for ivory and rhinoceros' horns, and all kinds of

woolen and cotton cloths, cloaks and tunics, shawls and sashes,
dyed with brilliant colours and broidered with gold. And all
this they did cheerfully and even joyfully, because it was for
the sake of the king. Benadam soon become accustomed
to this new life. Though at first it seemed strange to him,
the newness wore away, and he began to think that the people did no more than their duty in lavishing so much affection and loyalty upon him. Many happy weeks passed by
and even months without any interruption to his pleasure.
The fields were always clean and well kept, the barns and
storehouses full ; ships came often into port laden with rich
cargoes ; the officers obeyed the king's slightest wish ; wealth
and beauty were all round about him. He forgot that he had
once been a servant himself and that he had marvellously
escaped a terrible death. He only thought of the moment so
full of happiness, and believed that his joys would last for
ever.

One day there was a great commotion in the city. A
man had been seized by the king's guard, a strange man,
trying to force his way into the royal palace. They brought
him before the king to see what he would do with the
intruder. As he was being brought in, the wise counsellors
of Benadam besought him to banish the stranger from his
dominions ; " for," said they, " he is a dangerous-looking
man and is here for no good purpose." The prisoner stood
before the king, who started on his throne at the sight of
him. " Is it you Deror?" he cried ; " I thought you had
gone down into the lowest depths of the sea. Why did you
not stay there?" Deror laughed gently, for it was he, and
answered " The sea has cast me up, King Benadam, to be
useful to you. Am I not your own old servant, though I
have made mistakes in the past ? Trust me yet again and I

will serve you faithfully." The old counsellors whispered in the ear of the king, "Trust him not. He ruined you before, and will surely ruin you again." But Benadam thought he was secure and that, even if he wished, Deror could do him no harm; so he said, " Let him live and remain on the island. He is a useful and a bold man, and I will see him so rarely that his boldness will bring me no danger." The officers thought otherwise, and would fain have killed or banished the captain, but feared that in doing so they would grieve the king whom they loved. Thus Deror took up his abode near the royal palace.

It was true, as Benadam had promised, that he did not see Deror often, but whenever they met a great change took place in the king. Whatever Deror may have put into the monarch's head, it made him dissatisfied and petulant and even angry. The most watchful care, the most constant attention and readiness to supply all his wants, the richest gifts and most perfect obedience only irritated the king whom everybody sought to serve. Sometimes by Deror's advice he would lay great burdens upon the people and so aggravate them by his forgetfulness of their devotion that there was danger of a rebellion in the city. A rebellion there would certainly have been had not Deror's idle and wicked career been cut short. It happened in this way. Deror had, in his visits at Court, narrowly observed all the chief officers of Benadam's household and their attendants, and there was one person, an attendant and trusted servant of the first officer of the state, whom he had watched and taken every opportunity to meet. He had evidently found out something about this attendant, for whenever he saw him a scowl would come upon his bold handsome face. One day at last they met alone in front of the palace gates where the king could see them.　At once he saw Deror spring like a wild beast upon the quiet man to whom he had hitherto paid little attention.　He called his guard, and himself ran hastily to the spot.　The guards separated the two struggling men, but not before the marks of Deror's fingers were deep in his opponent's throat, and Deror's right leg was broken by the guard who fell upon and overpowered him. Benadam went up to the half strangled man with whom Deror had been fighting.　His turban had fallen off in the fray and his cloak been torn from his shoulders.　Benadam looked him in the face and lo, it was Hosah the helmsman, whom Deror had thus tried a second time to kill.　He soon old his story, how he had reached the island before Benadam and had taken up his abode with those who first greeted the new found king and placed the crown upon his brow.　Then Benadam, king though he was, tenderly embraced his old friend who had never done him aught but good, and ordered Deror to be put to death.

Meanwhile the wicked captain was suffering great pain from his broken leg.　He raved like a madman and fought with those who tried to bind him.　At last he found that he was helpless and became quiet as a little child.　The guards led him into the king's presence to hear the sentence of death from his own lips.　When the king saw his sad and helpless state and the tears that fell from his eyes, and when he heard his prayers for mercy and promises of good conduct, he was moved and wished that he had spared him. He was glad therefore when Hosah knelt before him, joined his prayers to those of his old enemy and vouched for Deror's good conduct in the future.　" He shall live," said Benadam, "on one condition, and that is that henceforth he shall be Hosah's servant and do nothing without his permission." The wounded captain gladly promised, and Hosah took him to his home, where he bound up the broken leg and laid his former foe upon his own couch. Thus peace came again to the island. The king was joyous and thankful and kind, the nobles rejoiced, and the people went about their labours with glad cheerfulness. In a short time Deror came out from his sick room leaning on Hosah's arm or driven about in the king's chariot, and when he was quite restored and only limped a little, he and Hosah went about the king's business with the royal officers, wisely ordering and helping in all that was to be done.

Four months had passed away on the island when Benadam, journeying through his kingdom, stood upon a mountain top and looked out upon the sea. All around he saw nothing but sea and sky, save in one point of the horizon, and there he thought he could discern a black spot where the heavens and the waters met. Hosah was with him, and, seeing his master look in that direction, he also looked steadily towards the same point. Being a pilot he was accustomed to sight far off objects with his keen glance. He saw that it was land and told the king so. "I must find out something about it," said Benadam, "as soon as we return to the palace." All the way home he thought of this distant land and wondered what coast it was. On his return he called his chief officers to him and inquired about this far off country. As soon as he spoke of it the officers began to sigh, and some of them to weep, while they answered : "Far be it from the king ever to set foot in that land." But one of the old counsellors, who had met him when he arrived on the island at the gate of the city, said : "My lord the king must know the history of this land in which he is, and of that which he has seen." Then Benadam

sat down and told the counsellor to say on. " This island,
my lord," replied the old man, "is inhabited by spirits in
bodily form who prayed once to the great God of Heaven to
give them a son of man to rule over them. God answered
their prayer and sent them such a son of man every year to
be their king. At the beginning of the year one such is cast
up upon the shore, naked and helpless as you were, and him
we take to be our sovereign. We clothe him with royal robes,
lodge him in a palace, nourish him with the good of the land,
and serve him with all our strength and substance. But when
the year is ended he must leave all these delights. We carry
him down to the harbour, strip off his royal robes and put
him into a bare and empty ship, which carries him over the
sea at which you have just been looking. The ship lands
him quickly upon the bleak spot you saw, which is a desolate
island, without building or tree or shrub, without well of water
or human being or living thing. There he wanders until he
perishes and his bones lie bleaching on the sand. Naked and
helpless you have come to us, and thus naked and helpless
you must return."

When Benadam heard the old counsellor speak these
words, his joy turned to bitterness. He smote upon his
breast and said, "O wretched man that I am ! In a few
short months another will come after me and enjoy all these
riches, and I, where shall I be ? Tell me, is there no escape?"
Then the old man answered : " There is no escape. It is the
lot of all the sons of men who reign here. The wise man said
" riches make themselves wings : they fly away as an eagle
towards heaven." But he has also said of the ant, that she
provideth her meat in the summer, and gathereth her food in
the harvest. Shall the ant be wiser than the king ? Shall not
he make provision for the future also ? There are ships

at the king's service, and we are all his subjects. Let him
employ them and us against the end of the year." These
sayings pleased Benadam as the former ones had grieved him.
He gathered his officers around the council board and listened
to the advice of each. They all recommended the exploration
of the distant desert island, and that ships full of all kinds of
provisions, of seeds and trees, of domestic animals, of building
materials, and of skilful workmen should go there at once
and land their cargoes in a suitable place for a royal domain.
Hosah and Deror offered their services and volunteered to
stay upon the desolate island and prepare everything for the
reception of the king. Benadam accepted their offer and that
of the old councillor's son who proposed to accompany them.
So that very day they began to load a large vessel, which so
far had been engaged in bringing articles of luxury for the
king's use, with seed of corn and grass, with growing vines and
flowering plants and trees for fruit and shade, with imple-
ments of husbandry, and with a large number of horses and
cattle, and labourers to till the ground. In a week the vessel
was ready and, amid the united prayers of king and people,
set sail under Hosah's skilful pilotage for the silent land.

The king's officers found the island just what they had been
led to expect, a dreary waste of treeless and waterless hill
and dale. At once the labourers were set to work digging in
the soil at the head of many valleys, and soon every little
company of well-diggers cried joyfully, " Look out for the
stream !" For out of the earth, in all the spots broken by their
spades, shot up great springs of water which flowed down
the centre of the valleys towards the sea. At first they
spread over the land in a shallow muddy tide, but, when the
force of the stream at the centre had worn a channel for
itself, the overflowing waters subsided into it and, after a

little, every valley was adorned with a clear sparkling brook
or rivulet. Upon the lately flooded land the seed was sown;
by the brook sides fruit trees were planted ; and vines on the
hills. As the labourers ploughed and dug the soil, new springs
and wells appeared, and wherever they were found verdure
and beauty soon followed. Some distance from the sea-shore,
Hosah and his companions discovered in the heart of the
hills a great circular valley many miles in diameter. This
they cultivated with special care, leaving a wide space in the
centre for a city such as that from which they had come.
Gardens were laid out and stocked with the flowering plants
and shrubs they had brought with them. Shade trees of
rapid growth lined the newly laid-out streets and filled the
parks, which soon began to be green under the influence of
the flowing water courses. The fields of corn even showed
promise of a rich harvest when Hosah and Deror and the
councillor's son set sail again for the dominions of Benadam.

Six months of the year had passed when they returned.
The king received them joyfully on their landing and
showed them, piled high upon the piers and landings, all the
materials he had been busy gathering for the desert island.
There were bricks and hewn stones, timber and carved wood
for building, with all kinds of furniture and drapery and
metal work, with horses and chariots and great store of
provisions. Many vessels besides the one Hosah brought
back were lying in the harbour waiting to carry these things
over the sea, and a thousand workmen were ready to embark
for the land their labours were to beautify. Great was the
joy of the men who had been left to cultivate the land and
tend the newly planted trees and vines and flowers, when,
looking out from the hill tops, they espied a great fleet of
ships making its way towards the once desolate shore a few

weeks later. Then, when the cargoes had been landed and placed on carriages and waggons, the newly made road to the site of the city in the central valley became a scene of busy life, as day after day the treasures of the old island were carried along it into the heart of the new. Next came the sound of hammer and saw and chisel. The city's walls rose rapidly with all their towers and gateways. The streets were no longer mere lines of levelled earth and stone laid out across the plain, but broad shady avenues between rows of shops and houses, with gardens all around them. And in the great parks the royal palaces, fairer in proportion and adornment than those of Benadam's island kingdom, raised their glowing pinnacles to the summer sky. When the eighth month ended the city's gates were hung, amid great rejoicing, to the sound of trumpets from the walls and the ringing of joy bells from the towers. Then Hosah and his companions returned with their empty ships to the dominion of the king.

They told the story of the once desolate island to Benadam and his people. The king was glad and the people were eager to go to the new land. So a proclamation was made that all who loved the king and wished to become inhabitants of the country to which he must go might sail thither with all their goods. All Benadam's wise counsellors, his best soldiers, his trusted attendants and faithful servants volunteered to go. The principal merchants and skilful workmen, the experienced husbandmen, and even the sailors came to the harbour begging for a passage. There was hardly room for them all and the property they brought with them in the fleet, although many ships had been added to it which used to trade only for the king's pleasure. As Benadam stood upon the shore watching the great fleet sail away he felt that all he loved best had gone, and that he hardly cared to stay behind. Back to

the palace he went with a few attendants, thinking of the time
when he should be compelled to leave his once happy home
and kingdom, no longer with fear but with joyful hope.   In
the meantime Hosah led the ships to the new island.   When
they arrived, the councillors and sailors, the friends and
merchants and servants and husbandmen gave a joyful shout
and could hardly believe their eyes at the wonders they saw.
The labourers and workmen who came to meet them told
them of new treasures they had discovered in the once barren
waste—of gold and silver and mines of gems and quarries of
marble that had been laid bare by the running water or by
the winds that blew away the surface sands.   They showed
them new flowers and grasses, seedling vines and trees such
as the old kingdom had never known, which had sprung out
of the earth where their seeds had long been hidden waiting
for the care of man.   Then all went to work.   To the husbandmen the lands were distributed ; the merchants took up their
abode in the shops and bazaars ; the sailors and shipwrights
dwelt by the sea and built new vessels against the king's
arrival : the councillors occupied the palaces of justice and
brought the people into order and happy ways of living ; the
servants prepared the royal palaces ; and the soldiers mounted
guard at the gates ; while the king's near friends built their
watch towers on the hills overlooking the sea and waited the
arrival of him whom they loved.   Ten months had passed
when Hosah and Deror and the chief councillor's son
departed to tell Benadam that all was ready.

The king met them when they landed. He looked pale and
tired.   He did not grumble at all : indeed he was kinder and
more grateful than ever, but it was easy to see that things
did not satisfy him as once they did.   He delighted now in
hearing about the new home and all the prosperity and hap-

piness there. Day after day when his public duties were over he would sit with his three friends and talk of what they had seen and done, and of the many friends who were there waiting for him. Sometimes he would be carried to a mountain top and look fixedly for hours over the sea to the little spot on the horizon which was soon to be his kingdom. He did not grieve now that another would soon take his place, but rather tried to make preparations for the coming of the next son of man, and gave costly gifts to those whose duty it was to meet him. As he knew that he could carry nothing away with him, he made his people happy by bestowing his wealth upon them. Thus he waited for the fatal day. It came at last, the last day of the twelfth month. The officers of state and all the people, dressed in their soberest and most gloomy attire, led him down to the harbour, clad in his royal robes. They bowed the knee before him for the last time, and then one officer took the crown from off his head, another stripped the royal robes from his shoulders, and a third put upon him the rags in which he had landed on the island a year before. Then they led him to a ship, low and narrow and black with sloping masts and many sails, and laid him in its bare unfurnished hold. Benadam shut his eyes. He did not see the ship, nor Hosah and Deror and the councillor's son who were with him though he did not know it, but he saw a great hand in which the very sea itself appeared to lie and he knew it for the hand that had saved him when shipwrecked on the Red Sea.

No ship ever passed through the waters like that ship. No sooner was Benadam, the naked and helpless and poor, safely on board, than the many sails filled till the masts bent, and away, like a lightning flash over the great upholding hand, the vessel sped and touched the far distant shore.

" Awake, awake, Benadam," cried Hosah and Deror and the councillor's son. The trumpets on shore and the joyous bells seemed to repeat the cry, " Awake." Down from the dark vessel came the poor man and saw it sink behind him. In a moment his rags were thrown off, and gorgeous raiment fit for the proudest emperor took their place ; sandals were on his feet, and a crown of blazing jewels decked his brow. With his companions he entered a chariot of costly workmanship ; and along the level highway, past green meadows and vineyards, orchards and gardens and fields of yellow corn, he sped towards the city. Half way his friends, who had come down from their watchtowers upon the hills, met him and fell upon his neck with such joy for him and them as he had never dreamt the heart of man could bear. There was room for them all in the chariot which was driven rapidly to the city's gates. What a welcome was there; such music, such glad faces, such shouts of " Long live the king !" Amid the blessings of many thousands Benadam passed through the shady avenues to the royal palace, and there began a new reign which has not ended yet and never will.

────

God, the great Father, has numberless servants in many parts of his wide dominions. Among them He chose one, the son of man, to be the object of his love. To him He gave no ship, treasure laden, but a priceless human soul and a world of beauty to rule over and enjoy. For the captain or chief director of the soul He appointed Freedom, and, for its guide, He gave him Trust. Trust would have the son of man to lean on God, but Freedom would have him confide in himself. There was a battle between the two in which Trust was beaten and left for dead. Then Freedom carried the soul upon the rocks of disobedience to God, and man's life was wrecked. Still God did not leave man. His Almighty hand held him up, and brought him, generation after generation, into a world full of beauty and riches and happiness. As a little child, all helpless, he comes into the world, a king tenderly cared for and waited upon by mother and father and friends, and all his life long he retains some real dominion over the creation of God. Again he is in danger of being led away by Freedom to care only for himself and for the present moment. Then Trust comes again before him, and the wise counsels of God's word and of His voice in the heart tell him what to trust. So if he refuses to listen to selfish will and submits his Freedom to God's Truth, he learns of the short life here and the endless life beyond the grave. Then, if he continues wise, he prepares for the future. All that he thinks and does is for the world that is invisible. His heart is there, and his treasure is where his heart is. The love of God the Father makes the world beyond the grave a second Garden of Eden instead of a dreary deadly waste. The love of God the Son builds it up with many mansions, and shows him his own house not made with hands, eternal in the heavens. And the love of God the Holy Ghost peoples it with those nearest his heart, with whom he is to enjoy in all its fullness the communion of the saints. The love which he gives, because he learns of the love of God who so loved the world, and the grace of the Lord Jesus Christ who died for sinners, and enjoys the fellowship of the Holy Ghost who bears with and speaks to the souls of unworthy men, shews itself in good deeds, every one of which is a ship of treasure sent over the sea of time to the life beyond. Soon comes the day of death, a day of joy and not of grief. Wealth and friends, fame and pleasure, everything that belongs to the earth is then put away, and alone, naked as he came into the world, he goes out of it. In a moment he is with his treasures ; and in the heavenly home, whither he is borne by the almighty hand which upholds the universe, he reigns a better and an eternal reign as a king and a priest to God.

THE END.

www.ingramcontent.com/pod-product-compliance
Lightning Source LLC
Chambersburg PA
CBHW030346270326
41926CB00009B/974